THE BOOK OF GENESIS

A Study Manual

by
CHARLES F. PFEIFFER

BAKER BOOK HOUSE
Grand Rapids, Michigan

Library of Congress Catalog Card Number: 58-8162

ISBN: 0-8010-6906-8

First Printing, June 1958
Second Printing, February 1960
Third Printing, September 1963
Fourth Printing, December 1965
Fifth Printing, June 1968
Sixth Printing, January 1970
Seventh Printing, November 1971
Eighth Printing, December 1973

PHOTOLITHOPRINTED BY CUSHING - MALLOY, INC.
ANN ARBOR, MICHIGAN, UNITED STATES OF AMERICA
1973

THE PURPOSE OF THIS MANUAL

In the form of an expanded outline, with interpretative comments, this *Study Guide* is designed to introduce the Bible student to the factual content of the first book of the Bible. Although written for the mature student, technical terminology has been kept at a minimum. References to the Hebrew are sparingly made by means of transliteration. Since there is no standard system of transliteration, the author of this Guide has attempted to use such characters in our alphabet as would provide the reader with no knowledge of Hebrew with an approximation of the original pronunciation. No attempt has been made to indicate emphatic letters or to introduce other phonetic distinctions. The Hebrew scholar will recognize the words discussed, and the reader who knows only the English Bible would be confused at the very attempt to write in a phonetically acceptable way.

The need for brevity of treatment has been kept in mind. Exegetical literature on the book of Genesis covers hundreds of volumes. As the "Book of Beginnings," Genesis touches upon every art and science known to man. No exegete can hope to be a master of every theme touched upon in the fifty chapters of this book. He must constantly acknowledge his dependence on those who are students of the natural sciences as he studies the early chapters of the book. That many questions must be left unanswered is a foregone conclusion. Although we acknowledge the Bible as an absolute, our knowledge of Scripture is relative. The student of Scripture, as the student of the natural sciences, must approach his task in humility. He is thankful for the clarity of the message of God's redeeming grace. He is conscious, however, that many academic questions which arise from his study of Scripture are, for the present, at least, unanswerable. To the immature student this appears frustrating. To the mature Christian, however, the very fact that he knows only "in part" and sees "through a glass, darkly" makes for a more conscious dependence on the Lord and a greater awe of Him who is infinite.

The approach to Genesis in this Guide is that of inspired history. God has acted in human history, and particularly in the history of Abraham's "seed." He has also raised up prophetic writers to record for future generations the sovereign acts of God, the divine purposes and promises.

Wherever possible we should seek to interpret Scripture in the light of its context. The widest context of the Book of Genesis is the culture of the lands of the "fertile crescent" — the area from the Persian Gulf, northwest through the Tigris-Euphrates Valley, and then south through Syria and Palestine to Egypt. All of this territory was touched by the life of Abraham.

Thanks to the work of the archaeologist, we are now able to describe in considerable detail the customs of Israel's neighbors during patriarchal times. The Code of Hammurabi, based on Sumerian antecedents, expresses the theoretical law of the eastern Fertile Crescent. The Nuzu tablets illustrate its practical outworking in the life of a community which had many customs which parallel those of the Patriarchal age. Mari, on the Euphrates, has helped us to understand the commercial life of the eighteenth and seventeenth centuries before Christ. Ras Shamra (ancient Ugarit) provides us with texts which describe the religion of Canaan during the time of the patriarchs. Egypt has yielded a wealth of hieroglyphic literature which illuminates those Biblical episodes taking place upon the land on the Nile. It has been our purpose to note significant episodes in Genesis which have parallels in the non-Biblical literature. A degree of interpretation is necessary in the use of such sources. The writer, for example, would consider any relationship between the *Enuma Elish,* the Babylonian creation story, and Genesis 1-2, to be most remote. The *Enuma Elish* is of no help in understanding the Biblical account of creation, except, of course, in providing a contrast between the pure monotheism of the Biblical account and the crass polytheism of that of Babylonia. The *Gilgamesh Epic,* however, has many points in common with the Biblical flood story, and no one could write about the Noahic deluge without constant reference to the Babylonian account. Here, too, the differences are as great as the similarities, but the details are such that there is no doubt that both accounts refer to the same flood.

Brief, but helpful, comments on the Book of Genesis will be found in:

> H. Alleman, in *Old Testament Commentary* (Muhlenberg Press) Philadelphia, 1948.

> Oswald T. Allis, *God Spake by Moses* (A brief, popularly written commentary on the Pentateuch. An appendix discusses the "interval" or "gap" theory of the relationship between Genesis 1:1 and 1:2.) (Presbyterian and Reformed Publishing Co.) Philadelphia, 1951.

E. F. Kevan in F. Davidson, *The New Bible Commentary*. (Eerdmans), Grand Rapids, 1953.

For more exhaustive treatments of Genesis, the student should have access to:

Franz Delitzsch, *A New Commentary on Genesis* (2 volumes) (T. & T. Clark), Edinburgh, 1899.

S. R. Driver, *The Book of Genesis (Westminster Commentaries)* (Methuen) London, 1948.

H. C. Leupold, *Exposition of Genesis* (2 volumes) (Baker) Grand Rapids, 1950.

John Skinner, "Genesis" in *International Critical Commentary* (Scribner's) New York, 1910.

For a topical or devotional treatment of Genesis the following may prove helpful:

Robert S. Candlish, *Commentary on Genesis* (Zondervan) Grand Rapids, n.d. (Reprint).

Charles R. Erdman, *The Book of Genesis* (Revell) New York, 1950.

W. H. Griffith Thomas, *Genesis: A Devotional Commentary* (Eerdmans) Grand Rapids, 1946.

Notes on the main topics of the book will be found in:
Albertus Pieters, *Notes on Genesis* (Eerdmans) Grand Rapids, 1943.

INTRODUCTION

NAME. Genesis, in the Hebrew Bible, is called *Bereshith*, "in the beginning," in accord with the Hebrew custom of naming a book by using its first word. The Greek translation, known as the Septuagint, made in the Egyptian city of Alexandria during the third and second centuries before Christ, gives the first book in the Bible the title *geneseos*, "origin," "source." The word occurs as the translation of *toledôth* in 2:4a, "This is the book of the *geneseos* of heaven and earth," and in the ten subsequent passages in which the same form is used. As this is the book of beginnings, the title "Genesis" is most appropriate. It was used in the Latin Vulgate and has been retained in many modern translations, including English. In the German Bible, however, Genesis is known as "The First Book of Moses," with other books of the Pentateuch successively numbered.

CONTENTS. The first part of the Hebrew Bible is known as the Torah, usually translated "law." The Hebrew concept of Torah is of wider scope than our English concept of law. Our word "instruction" approximates the Hebrew idea of Torah. This instruction may be contained in law codes, but it is also expressed in the inspired utterances of prophetic writers and in history as viewed as the revelation of God's sovereign acts in the guidance, protection, and discipline of His people.

Genesis is written in the form of history. It contains a series of historical records, each of which is headed by the words, "These are the generations *('elleh toledôth)* . . . (Genesis 2:4; 5:1; 6:9; 10:1; 11:10, 27; 25:12, 19; 36:1, 9; 37:2).

The narrative of Genesis begins with the record of creation and closes with the death of Joseph in Egypt. It progresses from the general to the specific, from world history to Israelite history. The first eleven chapters deal with mankind: his creation, fall, the flood which destroyed the race — except for Noah and his family — and the division of the world subsequent to the flood. These chapters are the introduction to the main theme of the book, the call of Abraham and God's dealings with him and his "seed" or descendants.

The history contained in Genesis, as in the other Biblical books, is not a chronicle of facts, but a series of specifically chosen episodes, genealogies or statistics, designed to exhibit the purposes of God with respect to his people at a given age. It forms the first stage in the fulfillment of the divine purpose in the Person of Jesus Christ and His redemptive ministry. The apostle John noted that he did not give a complete chronicle of the mighty deeds of the Son of God, but that he had selected certain events "that ye might believe that Jesus is the Christ, the Son of God" (John 20:31). The history contained in Scripture is never a bare recital of facts. It always has a purpose. Many facts are omitted, particularly those which do not have a bearing on the purpose of the writer. Because the purposes of God centered in the nation of Israel, the early history of mankind is outlined with a view to its bearing on the call of Abraham. The great nations of antiquity are mentioned as their histories and destinies are related to Israel. We can learn much about the Sumerians, the Babylonians, the Egyptians and the Hittites from extra-Biblical sources. The Bible, however, is a history of God's purposes concerning Abraham's "seed." Ultimately blessing comes through that seed to "all the families of the earth," but that part of the promise to Abraham is in the distant future as we study Genesis.

AUTHORSHIP. Although Genesis, with the other books of the Pentateuch, is traditionally ascribed to Moses, the name of Moses does not appear in the first book of the Bible. In view of the claims to Mosaic authorship of the subsequent books, the significant position of Moses as lawgiver and mediator of the covenant between God and Israel at Sinai, and the absence of tradition concerning any other author of Genesis, the consent of the ancient Jewish scholars and the testimony of the Christian church to the Mosaic authorship of the Pentateuch is worthy of respect.

When we state our belief in the Mosaic authorship of Genesis, however, we do not mean to imply that every word in the book was either dictated by God to Moses, or written at the initiative of the lawgiver himself. Written records had been preserved for at least a millennium and a half before the Mosaic age, and it is likely that Moses had access to written records which had been carefully preserved from a more remote antiquity. The fact that Moses had training in all the "wisdom of the Egyptians" (Acts 7:22), is evidence of the way in which he was providentially prepared for his ministry. An educated Egyptian of the time would have been familiar with the cuneiform writings of Mesopotamia as well as the hieroglyphs of Egypt.

Biblical writers frequently quote the sources of their material. The "Book of the Wars of the Lord" is specifically quoted (Numbers 21:14). Perhaps the form *'elleh toledôth* reflects the existence of genealogical tables or other materials which were in due time incorporated into Genesis.

It is probable that much of the pre-Mosaic history had been preserved orally. Most scholars consider the Song of Lamech (Genesis 4:23-24) to be the first poem in the Bible. It was doubtless passed on by oral tradition from generation to generation until Moses, under the guidance of the Holy Spirit, incorporated it into the book of Genesis.

The recognition of the Mosaic authorship of the Pentateuch does not deny the possibility, or even probability of later editorial revision. Place names may be modernized in order to make them intelligible to a later generation. Joshua, the "minister" and successor of Moses, may have written the account of Moses' death recorded in the last chapter of Deuteronomy. The Jewish tradition of the part Ezra played in the preservation of Scripture may reflect a final editing after the return from Babylon.

Admitting the probability of both pre-Mosaic and post-Mosaic elements in the Pentateuch, it is still necessary to assert the Mosaic authorship of the Pentateuch vis-à-vis those writers who date it late in the history of Israel. The school associated with the name of Julius Wellhausen considered the Torah to have been written at a period subsequent to that of the writing prophets. Most of it was dated during or subsequent to the Babylonian captivity. The use of the divine names, and other literary criteria were used in a critical reconstruction of the Pentateuch, or Hexateuch (the five Mosaic books plus Joshua). The religion of Israel was considered to be an evolutionary development, and the early Biblical writings were assumed to be the compilation of a series of redactors who preserved the traditions of Israel by editing, in a rather crude way, the various documents which the school confidently identified as E (The Elohist), J (The Jahvist), P (the Priestly Code), and D (the Deuteronomist). The list was expanded as other sources were identified.

Contemporary Old Testament studies have been characterized by a more conservative approach to Old Testament historical matters. The patriarchal age is no longer dismissed as myth and legend. The Amarna Letters, discovered in Egypt in 1887, the clay tablets from Nuzu and Mari in Mesopotamia, and the Canaanite literature discovered since 1929 at Ras Shamra (ancient Ugarit), all tend to place the Biblical records in a historical framework which we know to be true to fact. The

Wellhausen approach to the Scriptures has been either rejected *in toto* by modern scholars, or so modified as to make it hardly recognizable.

Emphasis has more recently been placed on oral tradition as the means for the preservation of the records of ancient Israel. The Scandinavian scholars have been pioneers in this field. While many problems are still unresolved, the emphasis on oral tradition has exercised a wholesome check on the so-called documentary hypothesis, which was considered one of the "assured results" of the Biblical criticism of an earlier generation.

The evangelical Christian is free to admit the existence of both written and oral traditions which were embodied in the Mosaic writings. He insists, however, that the Holy Spirit imparted to their human author that discrimination which enabled him to choose that which was both true and a necessary part of sacred Scripture. Similarly those editorial additions to the Mosaic writings, after the death of Moses, are equally inspired with the words which Moses himself wrote.

OUTLINE OF THE BOOK OF GENESIS

I. THE HISTORY OF MANKIND (Chaps. 1—11)

A. Creation (1—2)

1. The Creation of the Universe (1:1-2)
2. The State of This Creation (1:2)
3. The Seven Days (1:3—2:3)
4. The Details of Man's Creation (2:4-7)
5. Eden: God's Provision for Man (2:8-15)
6. The Tree of the Knowledge of Good and Evil: Man's Test (2:16-17)
7. Woman: Man's Complement (2:18-25)

B. The Temptation and Fall of Man (3:1—4:15)

1. The Tempter — the Serpent (3:1)
2. The Means of Temptation (3:1-5)
3. The Response to Temptation (3:2, 3, 6)
4. The Results of the Fall (3:7-8)
5. The Seeking God (3:8-13)
6. The Curse and the Promise (3:14-19)
7. Eve — the Mother (3:20)
8. Garments Provided (3:21)
9. Expulsion from the Garden (3:22-24)

C. Cain and Abel (4:1-16)

1. Their Birth (4:1-2)
2. Their Occupations (4:2)
3. Their Sacrifices (4:3-7)
4. Cain Murders Abel (4:8)
5. Cain's Punishment (4:9-15)

D. Cain and His Posterity (4:16-24)

1. Cain's Abode (4:16)
2. Cain's Wife (4:17)
3. The First City (4:18)
4. The First Polygamy (4:19)
5. The First Arts and Crafts (4:20-22)
6. The Song of the Sword (4:23)

E. Seth and His Posterity (4:25—5:32)

1. The Birth of Seth: A New Beginning (4:25-26)
2. The Descendants of Seth (5:1-32)

5. The Promise of an Heir (15:1-21)
   a. Abram's Fear (15:1-3)
   b. God's Response (15:4-5)
   c. Abram's Faith (15:6)
   d. The Solemn Covenant (15:7-17)
6. The Birth of Ishmael (16:1-16)
   a. Sarai's Suggestion (16:1-3)
   b. Contention between Hagar and Sarai (16:4-6)
   e. The Extent of the Promise (15:18-21)
   c. Hagar's Flight (16:7-8)
   d. The Message of the Angel (16:8-12)
   e. The Response of Hagar (16:13-16)
7. The Covenant with Abram-Abraham (17:1-27)
   a. The Theophany (17:1)
   b. The Promise (17:2-8)
   c. The Obligation (17:9-14)
   d. The Son To Be Born to Sarai-Sarah (17:15-22)
   e. The Obedience of Abraham (17:23-27)
8. The Destruction of Sodom and Gomorrah (18:1—19:38)
   a. The Visit of the Angels (18:1-16)
   b. God's Revelation concerning Sodom (18:17-22)
   c. Abraham's Intercessory Prayer (18:23-33)
   d. The Angels Rescue Lot (19:1-23)
   e. The Destruction of Sodom (19:24-29)
   f. Lot and His Family (19:30-38)
9. Abraham and Abimelech of Gerar (20:1-18)
   a. Abimelech Takes Sarah (20:1-2)
   b. God's Warning to Abimelech (20:3-7)
   c. Abimelech Confronts Abraham (20:8-13)
   d. Abimelech's Generosity and Blessing (20:14-18)
10. Isaac and Ishmael (21:1-21)
    a. The Birth of Isaac (21:1-7)
    b. The Mockery of Isaac by Ishmael (21:8-10)
    c. The Expulsion of Hagar and Ishmael (21:11-21)
11. Alliance between Abraham and Abimelech (21:22-33)
12. The Offering of Isaac (22:1-19)
    a. The Test (22:1-2)
    b. The Obedience (22:3-10)
    c. The Divine Provision (22:11-14)
    d. The Divine Blessing (22:15-19)
13. The Genealogy of Nahor (22:20-23)
14. The Death and Burial of Sarah (23:1-20)

11

I *The History of Mankind* (Chaps. 1—11)

A. (1—2) Creation.

1. The Creation of the Universe (1:1-2). The Bible begins with the simple yet profound statement that God *('Elohim)* is the creator of all that exists. It is the purpose of the inspired writer to focus our attention upon God as the source of all things. It is significant that *'Elohim* is a plural form, although interpreted as singular throughout the Old Testament — perhaps suggesting plurality in unity.

No hint is given concerning the date of creation. We simply read, "in the beginning." The relationship between 1:1 and the remainder of the chapter has been interpreted in varying ways. Some see in 1:1 a part of the creative activity of the first day. Others suggest a gap between 1:1 and 1:2, making the subsequent seven days a period of re-creation. A third view suggests that 1:1 describes an original creation preliminary to the work of the six days.

In creation God calls matter into existence, and endows it with fixed properties and laws. This act of creation is instantaneous. Natural processes are only possible after matter, with its laws and properties, is brought into being.

The terms "heaven and earth" are equivalent to the word "universe." Opposites in Scripture frequently signify totality (cf. "the dead, small and great" (Revelation 20:12), meaning all of the dead; ability "to go out and come in" (I Kings 3:7), ability to do anything). God is the creator of things material and things immaterial. Angelic beings and men were created by Him, and are subject to Him. It is noteworthy that, after the statement of the creation of the entire universe, the attention of the writer is focused on "the earth." Although the earth may be an infinitesimally small fraction of the universe, it is the scene of God's special creation, man, and of God's act of condescending love, the redemption of fallen man.

2. The State of This Creation (1:2). The creation is here described as formless, empty, dark, and fluid. Those who hold to the gap hypothesis suggest that this condition is the result of a cataclysmic judgment, perhaps involving the fall of the angels. The terms, "without form" and "void," however do not imply

anything morally evil. They describe the condition of the created universe prior to the activity of the six creative days in which the waters are separated and the land appears, giving "form" to the earth. The creation of animal life and man fills the "void" or emptiness of the original creation. The statement that "darkness was upon the face of the deep" is an additional indication of the incomplete and unfinished state of the earth.

The Spirit of God moving upon the face of the waters anticipates the work of the Spirit in the six creative days. The presence of the Spirit insures that God's purposes for the earth will be realized (cf. Isa. 45:18).

3. The Seven Days (1:3—2:3). The term "day" is used in Genesis 1 and 2 in various senses: (a) the light part of the day, in contrast to the night (1:5); (b) the full period of creation, including the six "days" (2:4); and (c) the creative "days" themselves. Opinion differs whether these corresponded to our days of twenty-four hours, or were indeterminate periods of time, or days of "dramatic vision" in which Moses is pictured as the recipient of the story of creation in a series of divine revelations spread over six days. The formula "evening and morning" is stressed by those who insist that the days are twenty-four hour periods. Those who believe that indeterminate periods of time are involved stress the fact that the sun, moon, and stars, ordained to measure time, do not appear until the fourth "day." It is also regarded as significant that no reference is made to the end of the seventh day. Any view accepted must be such as to allow the Biblical account of creation to stand as God's infallible word.

The oft repeated "And God spake . . . and it was so" tells us that everything came into being at God's Word. "He spake and it was done" (Ps. 33:9). This does not deny the operation of natural laws. In fact, together with the creation of the natural world, God established those natural laws with which He actively controls all things to this day.

The work of the six creative days falls into two corresponding divisions:

Works of Division	*Works of Quickening and Adorning*
1st Day, Light	4th Day, Sun, Moon, and Stars
2nd Day, Air and Sea	5th Day, Birds and Fish
3rd Day, Land and Plants	6th Day, Animals and Man

The work of the creative days is outlined as follows:

1st Day — Light (1:3-5). This light is distinct from that which later radiated from the sun. It dispelled the darkness which enshrouded the deep. Creation proceeds in an orderly fashion. Light forms the necessary first step in creation, for without light the world as we know it could not exist.

2nd Day — Air and Sea (1:6-8). The term "firmament" may be rendered "expanse." Before this creative act there was no clear expanse between the waters on the surface of the earth and the water vapor in the air above. The atmosphere itself is a part of God's creation.

3rd Day — Land and Plants (1:9-13). At God's word order is brought into what before was chaotic. Waters are brought together to form seas, and continents appear. "Let the earth bring forth . . ." here points to mediate creation. The recurring phrase "after its kind" expresses the thought "in all their varieties." Differences between groups and variation within groups seem to be accounted for by this formula.

4th Day — Sun, Moon, and Stars (1:14-19). The heavenly bodies are designed to illuminate the earth and to mark the divisions of time. Our English word "month" is related to the word "moon."

5th Day — Birds and Fishes (1:20-23). These fill the "air and sea" created on the second day. Here for the first time animal life appears. Each is adapted to the elements which God intended it to inhabit.

6th Day — Animals and Man (1:24-31). Here again we may have a reference to mediate creation: "Let the earth bring forth. . . ." If so, this in no way detracts from God's honor. God speaks the word that enables the earth to bring forth (Leupold). The animal life created on the sixth day is of higher class than that on the fifth day. Creation looks to man as its climax.

Man's creation differs from that of the animals in that he is made "in the likeness and image of God." This points to the dignity of man. After God's likeness man is an intelligent being, endowed with a will and a moral nature. After God's likeness man is to exercise dominion over the rest of creation (1:26,28). The subsequent entrance of sin blurred this likeness and rendered him impotent to fully carry out this purpose. In Christ, as the second Adam and the representative man, God's purposes are realized. Compare Hebrews 2:6-9 with Psalm 8.

17

The plural in the expression, "Let us make men . . ." in the light of divine revelation in the rest of Scripture undoubtedly alludes to the plurality in unity previously expressed in the word *Elohim.* This is further emphasized by the plural "Let *us* make man in *our* image after *our* likeness," followed closely by the singular, "So God created man in *his* image. . . ."

Here is related the institution of marriage (1:27b,28a) which is given in more detail in chapter 2.

After having read six times that God saw that what He had created "was good" (1:4,10,12,18,21,25), we read that "God saw *all* that He had made and behold it was *very* good," leaving us with no doubt as to the perfection of God's creation as it originally came into being at His divine word.

7th Day — The Sabbath (2:1-3). The sabbath marks the completion of God's creative acts. The vegetable and animal creation was designed to propagate itself, hence the creation may now be considered complete. God is not pictured as forsaking His creation, however. He is the source of life, and all life, whether produced by direct creation or natural generation, has its source in Him. The six days of creation are followed by the day of rest. This is not to be thought of as a rest required after exhaustion. It was, in the words of Allis, "the complacent resting which follows a finished task." This day of rest was sanctified, or hallowed as a memorial to the finished creation. Its observance was enjoined by the Mosaic law (Exodus 20:8-11). The Christian church observes the first day of the week as a memorial to the resurrection of Christ and the completion of the work of redemption.

4. The Details of Man's Creation (2:4-7). After the general account of the origin of all things (1:1-2:3), the sacred historian focuses our attention specifically on man. This section (2:4-25) is often called a second creation account. It is better, following Kevan, to regard the second passage as a sequel to the first. The thought proceeds from the creation of the universe (1:1) to the earth and all its occupants (1:1—2:3) to mankind, the crown of creation (2:4-25).

In 2:4a we meet for the first time the form *elleh toledoth,* "these are the generations of . . ." or "this is the story of. . . ." This phrase occurs eleven times in the book of Genesis (2:4; 5:1; 6:9; 10:1; 11:10, 27; 25:12, 19; 36:1, 9; 37:2). In each case the form *'elleh toledôth* introduces a new section of history.

The name Yahweh (popularly, but erroneously, pronounced Jehovah) appears for the first time in 2:4. The Creator is named

Yahweh Elohim. *Elohim* is the more general divine name. It is used of God as the Creator and moral Governor of the universe. It is equivalent to our word God, or god (s). The gods of the heathen are termed *elohim,* but never *Yahweh. Yahweh* is the distinctive name of the God (*'Elohim*) of Israel. It is used in those passages which stress the covenant between *Yahweh* and his people Israel. Historically, the Jews refrained from pronouncing *Yahweh,* the so-called tetragrammaton, pronouncing in its stead the word *Adonay,* Lord. The High Priest is said to have pronounced it on the Day of Atonement, during the Temple service, whereupon the people prostrated themselves and exclaimed, "Blessed be His Name whose glorious kingdom is forever and ever." Since the destruction of the Temple, the name has not been used at all.

Since the time of the French physician Jean Astruc (b. 1684) many Biblical scholars have attempted to use the divine names as criteria for dividing the pentateuch into various documents which are thought to have been edited by those who have put it into its present form. Astruc assumed that Moses used these earlier documents, but later scholars reduced Moses to a legendary figure and denied to him any real part in the authorship of the books ascribed to him. Although still widely held, the so-called "documentary hypothesis" does not enjoy the favor it did a generation ago. The use of divine names in non-Biblical literature, notably that of Ugarit, is strikingly similar to that of the Bible. Neither variation in names nor combined names can serve as satisfactory criteria for identifying documents.

There is no *a priori* reason for denying to Moses the use of earlier writings. Numbers 21:14f. quotes a fragment of poetry from "The Book of the Wars of the Lord." The *toledôth* of Genesis may be gathered from cuneiform tablets or other sources. Inspiration does not imply dictation, but includes the divine guidance of the human writers so that they produce the sacred Scriptures in the form in which God wants them produced.

In 2:5 two deficiencies are noted in the created world: (1). "The Lord God *(Yahweh 'Elohîm)* had not caused it to rain upon the earth" and (2.) "There was not a man to till the ground." Verses six and seven show how these deficiencies are met.

The word rendered "mist" *('ēdh)* (verse 6) has puzzled the commentators. It has been equated with an Assyrian word meaning "the overflow of a river." The Septuagint translators render the word as *pēgē* ("spring"). Leupold suggests that a

19

threefold process is here envisioned: the rising of the mists, their condensation, and the regular falling as rain. This would be the account, then, of the removal of the first deficiency noted in verse five.

Verse seven describes the creation of man (cf. 1:27). Man's relationship to both heaven and earth is described. His body is from the dust of the ground, but his breath, or life, was imparted directly by God. Physically, man has much in common with the animal creation. Man alone, however, is created "in the image of God."

5. Eden: God's Provision for Man (2:8-15). Unfallen man was placed in a garden and assigned a simple task — tilling the garden. Of the four rivers mentioned in connection with the Garden of Eden, two are well known. The Hiddekel (Akkadian *Idiqlat*) is the Tigris which, with the Euphrates, forms the area of Mesopotamia. The Pison and the Gihon are not known. Verse 13 states that the Gihon "flows around the whole land of Cush (Ethiopia, A.V.)" Cush usually refers to Ethiopia. In this context it may refer to the land of the Cassites, a people that succeeded in conquering Babylonia and establishing a dynasty there from about 1600 to 1150 B.C.

Among the many trees which grew in the garden, verse 9 specifies two as of particular significance: the tree of life, and the tree of knowledge of good and evil. The tree of life was designed to confirm man in the possession of physical life, and to render physical death an impossibility. Because of man's sin, it never came to be used. Man was expelled from the garden, after his sin "lest he put forth his hand and take also of the tree of life, and eat, and live forever" (3:22-23).

6. The Tree of the Knowledge of Good and Evil: Man's Test (2:16-17). Man was blessed by God in the beautiful Garden of Eden, but man had one responsibility: obedience to the express command of God. God chose a tree as the means whereby Adam could be tested. We need not assume any magic quality in the tree. It was the fact of disobedience which would mar man's fellowship with God.

7.Woman: Man's Complement (2:18-25). Man had the ability of speech, and exercised it in giving names to the animals which God had created. Being essentially different from them, however, man could find no satisfying companionship with the animals. He had need of a companion like himself. Woman, created from man, is a reminder that male and female are originally one. Jesus emphasized this oneness in declaring the sacredness of the marriage relationship (cf. Matthew 19:5). A "help meet for him" is an archaic way of saying, "A helper, suitable for him." Life is realized in its fullest dimensions when man and woman dwell together in that unity which God purposed and established.

B. (3:1—4:15) The Temptation and Fall of Man.

Of man, as of the rest of creation, God expressed His pleasure in the verdict "very good" (1:27, 31). Man was created an upright being with the capacity for obedience. Man was also created as a moral being, and as such, he was subjected to a test. The place of man's temptation was the finest imaginable. In the beautiful Garden of Eden, God had placed everything that man could wish for his well-being. Nothing was lacking in man's environment. As a test, however, man was subject to one prohibition. He might "freely eat" of all of the trees of the garden save one, the "tree of the knowledge of good and evil."

1. The Tempter — the Serpent (3:1). The serpent is called "more subtle than all the beasts of the field." The Hebrew word *'arûm,* "subtle," conveys the idea of shrewdness as well as craftiness. In some contexts *'arûm* is a complimentary term, signifying "prudence."

It is clear that Satan used the serpent to accomplish his evil purpose (cf. John 8:44; Romans 16:20; II Corinthians 11:3; I Timothy 2:14; Revelation 12:9; 20:2). It is more than an inference that Satan is to be identified with the serpent, for Revelation 20:2 speaks of "the dragon, that old serpent, which is the Devil, and Satan."

2. The Means of Temptation (3:1-5). The serpent began his attack by lodging doubts in the woman's mind concerning the reality of God's prohibition (3:1). He implied that God was seeking to withhold some good from mankind. Thus both the word and the benevolence of God were challenged.

3. The Response to Temptation (3:2, 3, 6). The correct response to temptation is given in James 4:7b, "Resist the devil and he will flee from you." When Satan attempted to divert Jesus from the path which led to Calvary by offering "all the kingdoms of the world," Jesus replied, "Get thee hence, Satan" (Matthew 4:10a). Eve, however, showed a willingness to come to terms with the tempter. In modifying God's warning, "thou shalt die" (2:18) to a less emphatic "lest ye die" she showed a willingness to trifle with God's command. The tempter's out-

right denial of the Word of God (3:4) should have proved a warning, but Eve had permitted his insinuations to find a place in her heart. She looked upon the forbidden fruit, esteemed it desirable, ate of it, and gave it to her husband who also ate of it.

4. The Results of the Fall (3:7-8). The consequences of sin were both immediate and remote. Paul declares, ". . . in Adam, all die . . ." (I Cor. 15:22). Physical death is part of the penalty of sin. The consciousness of separation from God is a more tragic consequence.

A sense of shame caused Adam and Eve to make aprons of fig leaves to cover their nakedness. The body is to be honored as God's creation, but fallen man is tempted to abuse that which God has made as a means of blessing.

The approach of God (3:8), which normally would have filled them with joy, became a subject of terror to Adam and Eve. Transgression of God's commandment had resulted in estrangement from God Himself.

5. The Seeking God (3:8-13). The omniscient God did not bring immediate physical death upon His rebellious creatures. He approached them in grace and gave them an opportunity to declare their need. Instead of pleading for mercy, however, they began at once to make excuse. Adam blamed Eve, and implied that God was somewhat at fault ("The woman whom thou gavest to be with me," 3:12). The woman, disclaiming responsibility, blamed the serpent.

6. The Curse and the Promise (3:14-19). The woman, the man, and the serpent, were all guilty. The curse pronounced on the transgressors was three-fold:

a. The Serpent. The serpent was degraded. He was told that his "seed" would be the enemy of the "seed of the woman." The serpent would bruise the heel of the woman's seed, but the serpent's head would be bruised.

This *protevangelium* or first gospel is deemed the beginning of the line of Messianic prophecy. It looks forward to the advent of Jesus. Man had brought sin into the world, but Man (the "seed of the woman") would one day bring about the destruction of the Evil One. The tempter may appear, for a time, to have spoiled God's good creation, but the victory of God is assured in the first moments of man's history as a sinner. History was to follow a long, tortuous path, but "in the fulness of time," the Son of Man, the last Adam accomplished the defeat of Satan through His own death on the cross.

22

b. The Woman. The excuse of the woman was not accepted. Because she was responsible for her sin, the woman was assigned a place of subordination and suffering. Pain in child birth, and subjection to her husband would be her normal experience. It should be noted that woman's place in life can be one of honor and love. While the penal nature of punishment must not be minimized, it should also be emphasized that the wisdom of God assigned to fallen man and fallen woman those places in the economy of life which would produce blessing and satisfaction in lives of loving obedience to God.

c. The Man. Not an idle spectator, man is recognized as an active participant in the rebellion against God which constituted the first sin. Man is told that he will have to labor over thorny ground before it will produce its fruit. Man's life will be one of physical hardship before his body returns to the dust from which it came. However, labor is also a blessing to fallen man. Unable now to enjoy the bliss of paradise, he now has work to occupy his hands and mind.

7. Eve — the Mother (3:20). The penalty of sin was death. Yet in the midst of death, woman is given a name which means life. Eve is the English rendering of *ḥawah,* the Hebrew word "to live." Eve became the mother of all human beings. She also had the promise, implied in the curse upon Satan, that her "seed" would ultimately bring salvation to lost mankind.

8. Garments Provided (3:21). Fallen man had fashioned garments of fig leaves to cover his nakedness. God, however, provides coats of skins. No details are given concerning the manner in which the animals were slain to provide these garments. Some Bible students suggest that this verse marks the beginning of animal sacrifice. Franz Delitzsch notes: "This clothing is a foundation laid at the beginning, which prophetically points to the middle of the history of salvation, the clothing with the righteousness of the God-man, and to its end, the clothing with the glorified resurrection body in the likeness of the God-man" *(New Commentary on Genesis,* I, 171).

9. Expulsion from the Garden (3:22-24). The Tree of Life was the symbol of man's blessedness in the Garden of Eden. It reappears at the end of human history (Revelation 22:2; cf. 2:7). Rebellious man, however, cannot have access to the Tree of Life. He is prevented from returning to the Garden and commanded to till the ground. Angelic beings known as Cherubim prevent man from returning to his forfeited paradise.

Deprived of the enjoyment of the Garden, man is required to labor for his physical needs.

Scripture does not suggest the length of time which the Garden of Eden remained on the earth after the expulsion of Adam and Eve. For a time the Cherubim and a revolving sword-like flame prevented man from returning to his lost paradise. In time, however, the Garden and the Paradise which it represented became but a memory of a past golden age. The memory, however, served to quicken hope in a golden age yet to come, when sin would be banished and man would again dwell in unbroken fellowship with his Creator.

C. (4:1-16) Cain and Abel.

1. Their Birth (4:1-2). Cain was the first human born into the world, a son of Adam and Eve. His name is a play on the Hebrew word *qanah,* "to get, acquire." Eve exclaims, "I have gotten a man with (the help of) the Lord." His birth may have seemed a fulfillment of the promise of Genesis 3:15. Further details concerning the nature of the prophesied deliverer had not been revealed. A second child, Abel, was born. The Akkadian word *ablu* means "son," and the name of Abel may have had that significance. The Hebrew name, however, means "breath," "vapor," or "vanity." If the name is to be accounted for in this way, it is because the vanity of human existence had impressed itself on Adam and Eve. They had come to realize the results of sin in the created world.

2. Their Occupations (4:2). The years of the infancy and childhood of the two boys are quickly summarized. When they reached maturity they manifest differing tendencies in the matters of occupation and attitude toward God. Cain and Abel were engaged in the two most primitive occupations of mankind. As the younger brother, Abel was given the lighter task of caring for the flocks, while Cain labored in the cultivation of the soil.

3. Their Sacrifices (4:3-7). This is the first mention in Scripture of an act of sacrifice. The two brothers brought sacrifices appropriate to their vocations. Each is called a *minhah,* a gift or offering. There are significant differences, however. Cain is said to have brought of the fruit of the ground (apparently without selection), whereas Abel brought of the firstlings of the flock — the very best. The attitude of the worshipper is always important in the Biblical doctrine of sacrifice. Isaiah cries out, "Bring no more vain oblations *(minḥat shawe')"* (1:13). The epistle to the Hebrews (11:4) makes it clear that Abel's offering

24

was accepted because it was brought "by faith." Presumably Cain's offering was a perfunctory one. It was not offered in the right spirit, and it was rejected.

In the subsequent teaching of Scripture concerning the nature of acceptable sacrifice, much stress is placed on the shedding of blood (cf. Hebrews 9:22). This fact leads us to suggest that both Cain and Abel knew that a bloody sacrifice was necessary. Sacrifice, then, would not have been the spontaneous act of the first worshipers, but the subject of divine revelation. The faith of Abel (Hebrews 11:4) would have that revelation as its object. Cain's offering was rejected both because of the spirit in which it was offered and the unacceptable nature of the offering itself.

The means used to indicate God's acceptance of Abel's offering and rejection of that of Cain is not indicated. There is no textual warrant for the idea that Abel's offering was consumed by fire. Cain was, however, warned of the consequences of rebellion against God's will. Verse 7 seems to imply that Cain's countenance which was "fallen" because of his non-acceptance might yet be "lifted up" as a result of a change in attitude and action ("if thou doest well"). The verb translated "lifted up" (*nasa'*) also conveys the meaning of forgiveness. Sin is thought of as "lifted up," hence "removed" and the one who was burdened with sin is forgiven. Such was one possibility for Cain. Another, more terrifying one, was also possible. If he refused to "do well," sin, like a wild beast, was ready to pounce upon him and devour him. The worst punishment for sin is to be delivered into the power of sin. Sin, at first alluringly attractive, becomes a tyrant of a master. Cain was given the opportunity of gaining the mastery over sin, but he was mastered by it instead.

4. Cain Murders Abel (4:8). In the Masoretic Text we read, "And Cain spoke unto Abel, his brother." Many ancient versions, including the Septuagint, add "let us go into the field." In the field, Cain slew Abel. Of Adam's first two sons, one became a murderer, the other a martyr. The "seed of the woman" was not to enter the human race for many millennia.

5. Cain's Punishment (4:9-15). Cain met the Lord's question about Abel's whereabouts with the insolent rejoinder, "Am I my brother's keeper?" Judgment was quickly passed on the murderer. He was destined to live the life of a fugitive. Although his life was spared, he lived in constant terror. The "sign" which the Lord "set for Cain" is usually understood to be a

mark placed on him to distinguish him from others. It is possible to interpret the "sign" as a pledge, like the rainbow, given to assure Cain that God would preserve his life from possible adversaries. The text presupposes that other children were born to Adam and Eve, and that one of them might desire to avenge Abel's blood. Although judged for his sin, even Cain experienced the mercy of God.

D. (4:16-24) Cain and His Posterity

1. Cain's Abode (4:16). Having forfeited God's favor, Cain withdrew from the neighborhood of Eden, traveling eastward to "the land of Nod" ("wandering"). The land of Nod cannot be specifically located. It probably simply means a territory occupied by nomads, or wanderers.

2. Cain's Wife (4:17). Scripture makes it clear that many sons and daughters were born to Adam and Eve in addition to those named in the book of Genesis (cf. 5:4). Although marriage to the near of kin was forbidden in the Mosaic law (Leviticus 18:9), it was unavoidable in the earliest stages of the history of the race.

3. The First City (4:17). Nomadic life precedes that of the settled city-dweller. The building of the city marked a new stage in the development of civilization. The text does not state that Cain personally completed the city. It reads, literally, "And he was building *(boneh)* a city." Cain lived the life of a nomad, but he determined to build a city for his offspring. The first city was named after Enoch *(Hanok)*, a son of Cain, to be carefully distinguished from Enoch, son of Jered of the line of Seth. The name Enoch conveys the idea of dedication or commencement. The naming of a city after Enoch, who may be the one who completed it, marks a new cultural beginning.

4. The First Polygamy (4:19). Jesus makes it clear that, from the beginning, God's standard for marriage involved one man and one woman in a life-long relationship. The Scriptures record many instances of the violation of this principle, with tragic results.

5. The First Arts and Crafts (4:20-22). In the legendary literature of ancient peoples the arts and crafts are the inventions of the gods. Generally a specific deity is associated with each art or craft. In the Genesis record the arts and crafts are seen as human developments, produced by members of the line of Cain:

26

(a) Jabal — the "father" or originator of the pastoral life. Cain had been a keeper of sheep (4:2) but Jabal kept "cattle" — i.e. the larger domesticated animals.

(b) Jubal — the originator of instrumental music.

(c) Tubal-cain — the originator of metallurgy. The metals mentioned are copper and iron. The discovery of the use of metals forms an important step in the progress of civilization. It has been thought that meteoric iron was used before methods of mining and smelting iron were developed. Although the Iron Age is dated quite late in history, it is likely that rust has caused the remains of early iron utensils to disappear.

6. The Song of the Sword (4:23). This is the first bit of poetry quoted in the Bible. It was doubtless passed on by word of mouth for centuries before becoming a part of sacred Scripture. It is perhaps incorporated in this chapter because it illustrates so well the spirit of Cain.

The poem may be rendered:

> Adah and Zillah, hear my voice;
> Ye wives of Lamech, hearken unto my speech;
> For I have slain a man for wounding me,
> And a young man for bruising me;
> If Cain may be avenged sevenfold
> Truly Lemech seventy and seven fold.

This "Song of Lamech" follows the account of the forging of bronze and iron implements by Tubal-cain. It breathes an almost unbelievable defiance of God. God had declared that the one who would harm Cain would experience a seven-fold punishment (4:15). Lamech threatens that, by the strength of his own weapons he will extract a vengeance of seventy-seven fold. He can slay a man at the slightest provocation without fear of the consequences. Lamech's attitude is similar to that ascribed to Voltaire, who declared, "It is said that God is always for the big battalions." The spirit of Cain and Lamech has never been completely absent from human affairs.

E. (4:25—5:32) Seth and His Posterity.

1. The Birth of Seth: A New Beginning (4:25-26). The birth of Seth (meaning "placed" or "appointed") marks a fresh start, "another seed instead of Abel." The line of Cain had reached a climax of boastful and unrestrained violence in Lamech. Righteous Abel had been murdered.

In the days of Enos, son of Seth, we read that "men began to call upon the name of the Lord (Yahweh)." The reference is to public worship as distinguished from the private worship exhibited in Abel's offering. The name *Yahweh,* for which the Jews substituted *'Adônay,* "the Lord," is later used specifically for the God of Israel (cf. Exodus 3:13-15). He was worshipped by "men" however, before Israel comes into being as a distinct people. While he entered into covenant relations with Israel, his purposes and promises transcend all local and national considerations.

2. The Descendants of Seth (5:1-32). The longevity of the antediluvians has been the subject of much speculation, but theories that seek to redefine the term "year" have proved unsatisfactory. According to the theory of "lunar years" (i.e. months), Enoch would have been $5\frac{1}{4}$ years old at the birth of his son Methuselah. That the years refer to individuals rather than clans is clear from the fact that Noah is described as being 600 years old at the beginning of the flood.

The Sumerian King list gives a record of eight kings who reigned over ancient Sumer before the flood. That the Sumerian flood is the same as that described in Genesis is evident from a comparison of the Sumerian flood story with the Genesis account. The eight Sumerian ante-diluvians reigned a total of 241,200 years, according to the Sumerian genealogies. The oldest in the Bible (Methuselah) did not quite reach the age of 1000 (actually 962, cf. 5:20), but the oldest in the Sumerian list reigned 43,200 years.

It appears that the Sumerians, along with other peoples of antiquity, had within their corporate memory a recollection of an early period of history when life expectancy was much longer than it subsequently became. The natural tendency to exaggerate the unusual accounts for the fantastically large numbers in the Sumerian list.

The Bible is witness to the fact that, subsequent to the flood, life expectancy progressively declined until the "three score and ten" of Psalm 90 became the norm.

Although we have genealogies before the flood, we do not have chronologies. In many Old Testament genealogies a selective principle is applied. By tracing the genealogy recorded in Matthew 1 with its Old Testament references it will be noted that a genealogy need not present every link in the chain. The terms "son," "daughter," and "begat" have a much wider usage in the Semitic languages than they do in modern European tongues. It does not seem strange to us to read of Jesus as "son of David," although we realize that David lived a thousand years before Jesus was born of the Virgin Mary in Bethlehem.

The genealogy of Enoch is different from that of the others. Instead of a reference to Enoch's death we read that he "walked with God, and was not; for God took him" (5:24). In Hebrews 11:5 we are told that, living a life of faith, he was "translated" without passing through death. Enoch and Elijah are the two Old Testament figures whose exodus from this life was not by means of death.

The other names in the genealogy lived their lengthy life span and physically preserved the race by begetting sons and daughters. Enoch did that, too, for he was the father of Methuselah. Enoch, however, differed from the others in the spiritual orientation of his life. He lived a life of fellowship with God in an age which was becoming increasingly more decadent.

F. (6:1-8) Wickedness Increases.

The wickedness of man developed to the point where divine judgment in the form of the flood was inevitable. God explains, as preparation for the flood, the course of human history which brought about the destruction of the antediluvians.

1. Marriage of the Sons of God with the Daughters of Men (6:1-4). Two principal views have been held as to the identity of the "sons of God" who married the "daughters of men." In Job 1:6 the "sons of God" are clearly angels. The pre-Christian pseudepigraphal book of Enoch and the Jewish historian Josephus used the term in that sense. In recent times Franz Delitzsch held this view. Skinner, in the *International Critical Commentary* on Genesis, suggested that the reference to angels in Genesis 6 was a remnant of Hebrew mythology.

On the other hand, many Bible students identify the "sons of God" with the godly, or men of the line of Seth, and the "daughters of men" with the wicked, or women of the line of Cain. This view harmonizes with the statement of Jesus that the angels "neither marry nor are given in marriage" (Matthew 22:30). It should be remembered that the Genesis account does not simply state that angelic beings had illicit relations with mortals. The Scripture is clear that they took wives. The relationship was a permanent one. In the subsequent judgment of the flood there is no hint of judgment on angels. It is men who sin, and a race of men that perishes in the waters of the deluge.

The term translated "giants," *(nephilim)* in verse 4 is, literally, "fallen ones." In Numbers 13:33, spies returned to Moses reporting that they had seen *nephilim* in the Hebron area. This does not necessarily indicate that *nephilim* survived the flood. The Israelite spies knew of traditions of *nephilim* of great stature (*gigantēs* in the Septuagint). They identified the inhabitants of Canaan with these *nephilim*. There is no hint that the Canaanites had any relationship to angelic beings.

2. Declaration of Impending Judgment (6:3). God declares that His Spirit will not "strive with" or, as otherwise rendered, "abide in" man forever. Judgment will come after 120 years of further grace. This, rather than a reduction of life expectancy to 120 years, seems to be the meaning of verse 3b. No reference is made to angels. The flood is a judgment on fallen man.

3. God's Attitude toward Man (6:5-8). Anthropomorphic terms are used to describe God's attitude toward rebellious man. God is described as being grieved (cf. Eph. 4:30) that man continues to sin in spite of continuing mercy. The mention of God's repentance does not imply a change in the divine nature. God always loves righteousness and hates evil. When man turns from righteousness to evil he experiences that wrath which is God's normal reaction to sin. God's attitude toward sin and righteousness is always the same. A change is experienced by man when he moves from one sphere to the other.

Universal judgment found one exception, however. Righteous Noah was spared, and through him humanity was to find a new beginning.

G. (6:9—8:22) Noah Spared from Destruction by Flood.

Noah is described as a man of righteousness and integrity (*tsaddîq tamîm*). Although no concept of sinlessness is implied, Noah stands out as an exception to the degeneracy of the antediluvians.

1. Noah Builds the Ark (6:9-22). Godly Noah became the father of Shem, Ham, and Japheth before he was warned by God that divine judgment was to fall on mankind. He was then given explicit instructions for the building of the ark.

Noah's ark was a kind of covered raft, built of cyprus ("gopher") wood, 450 feet long and 75 feet wide (figuring 18 inches to the cubit.) Its three floors reached a height of 45 feet. Around the top of the ark was a *tsohar* or "light" (rather than "window") eighteen inches deep, designed to let in air and light. The ark was pitched to make it water tight.

The Babylonian flood story, found on the eleventh tablet of the Gilgamesh Epic, has some interesting parallels with the

Biblical record. The ark of the Gilgamesh Epic was in the form of a giant cube with a displacement of about five times that of Noah's ark. In both accounts the ark was pitched.

2. Noah Enters the Ark (7:1-10). God graciously invited Noah and his household to enter the ark which was designed to provide safety in the hour of judgment. Thus eight people were spared: Noah, his wife, his three sons, and their wives.

Seven of each of the clean animals were brought into the ark. Although the codification of the laws of clean and unclean animals took place at the time of Moses (Leviticus 11), sacrifices are mentioned in the earliest chapters of Genesis (cf. 4:3-4). Clean animals are probably to be identified with those which were used for sacrifice. Sacrifices were offered as soon as Noah and his family left the ark. To perpetuate the species, two of each of the unclean animals were also brought into the ark.

3. The Flood (7:11-24). Two factors are mentioned as producing the flood waters: heavy rains from above, and the "fountains of the great deep" from beneath. The latter may refer to earthquakes with accompanying tidal waves. Volcanic eruptions suddenly raising the ocean floor and the fall of giant meteorites into the sea are also suggested.

The Gilgamesh Epic makes the very gods fear the terrors of the flood:

The gods were frightened by the deluge,
And, shrinking back, they ascended to the heaven of Anu
    (the highest heaven).
The gods cowered like dogs
Crouched against the outer wall.

The Gilgamesh Epic, although referring to the same flood as that described in Scripture, does so in a polytheistic setting. The reason for the flood is the caprice of the gods rather than judgment on sin. That a cataclysm such as the flood should be remembered in the traditions of different peoples is to be expected. That it should be fitted into varying traditions is also quite understandable.

Considerable discussion has centered around the extent of the flood. Although the language of the Genesis account is universal, some have suggested that the flood was universal only as far as man's experience at the time was concerned. Since, it is assumed, man had not scattered all over the globe, a global flood was not necessary to accomplish the purpose of the flood. Whether universal or local it is clear that Noah and his family alone were preserved from judgment, and that mankind had a new beginning after the flood.

The events of the flood may be diagrammed thus:

Month	Day	Events	Number of Days
2	17	All enter the ark. God shuts the door. Rain falls. Floods pour in from the sea. The ark floats.	40
3	27	Rain stops. Floods keep pouring in and the water rises.	110
7	17	Ark touches bottom on top of high mountains. Waters stop rising. Water becomes stationary.	40
8	27	Waters begin to settle. They settle fifteen cubits in 34 days.	
10	1	Ark left on dry land. Waters continue to settle. Noah waits.	40
11	11	Noah sends out a raven. It does not return. Waters settle. Noah continues to wait.	7
11	18	Noah sends out a dove. It returns. Waters continue to settle. Noah waits.	7
11	25	Noah sends out a dove again. Dove returns with an olive leaf. Waters continue to settle. Noah waits.	7
12	2	Noah sends out a dove again. It does not return. Waters continue to settle. Noah continues to wait.	29
1	1	Noah removes covering, looks around. No water can be seen. Ground dries up. Noah continues to wait.	56
2	27	God opens the door. Noah and his family leave the ark.	
		Total time of flood	370

—Adapted from G. F. Wright in the
International Standard Bible Encyclopedia

4. The Subsiding of the Waters (8:1-14). While waiting for the waters to subside, Noah released a series of birds to determine the proper time to leave the ark. The raven, a carrion-loving bird that can stand inclement weather, was first released. Subsequently two doves were released, the second of which returned with evidence that the waters had abated. The Gilgamesh

Epic also describes the release of three birds, a dove, a swallow, and a raven.

When the waters had subsided it was found that Noah's ark had come to rest on the mountains of Ararat, Assyrian *Urartu*, or Armenia. A specific peak is not mentioned.

5. Noah Leaves the Ark (8:15-22). On leaving the ark, Noah built an altar and offered a burnt offering to God. The Gilgamesh Epic mentions a similar detail. In crass polytheistic language, it pictures the gods, hungry as a result of being deprived of sacrifices during the time of the flood, gathering like flies around the sacrificer.

Following the sacrifice which Noah made, God pledged that the seasons would follow one another in orderly succession, without the inevitable changes made by a cataclysmic judgment. Individual sin will, of course, be punished, but the flood will not be repeated. God designated the rainbow as the visible sign of this covenant (9:12).

H. (9:1-17) After the Flood: A New Beginning.

Noah and his sons became the head of a new race. Certain of God's commandments to Adam were repeated with some modification.

1. God's Commands to Noah (9:1-7). Noah, like Adam, was commanded to "be fruitful and multiply and replenish the earth." It is noteworthy that the words "and subdue it" (cf. 1:28) are not part of the command to Noah. Its omission is a reminder that sinful man is limited in his ability to bring nature into his service. The age of science has helped all of us, but we must remember the limitations of scientific achievement. Only in Christ does man reach the fulness of his potentiality (cf. I John 3:2).

Man was authorized to use the animal creation for food, but certain restrictions were stipulated. Blood, symbolic of life and used in sacrifice to God, was not to be eaten. Human blood, as distinguished from animal blood, must not be shed. Man was created in the image of God. Although that image is marred by sin, human life is still to be regarded as sacred.

The penalty for murder is death (9:6). Human society must function in a framework of law. The willful murderer must not be permitted to endanger the lives of others. It is because life is reverenced that the death penalty is prescribed for the murderer.

2. God's Covenant with Noah (9:8-17). The rainbow was made a token or sign of the fact that God would remember

His covenant of grace with Noah. Following a storm, the rainbow in the sky would serve as a reminder that a flood would never again destroy mankind. God pledged Himself to faithful remembrance of His covenant.

3. Noah's Drunkenness: Blessings and a Curse (9:18-27). This is the first reference in Scripture to intoxicating beverages. Some interpreters suggest that Noah was the first to cultivate the vine and, for this reason, was ignorant of the intoxicating effect of its fruit. This is an argument from silence, however. It seems clear that the sacred historian wishes to imply guilt on Noah's part. That righteous Noah should be overtaken by the sin of drunkenness serves as a warning to the subsequent ages of mankind.

Ham and his son Canaan appear to have vulgarly looked upon Noah, whereas Shem and Japheth showed him proper filial reverence. This fact became the basis for a curse upon Canaan, and blessings on Shem and Japheth.

a. Canaan was to become a "servant of servants," i.e., in Hebrew idiom, the lowest form of a servant. Canaan is the progenitor of the Canaanites, the inhabitants of Canaan who were dispossessed by the armies of Israel under Joshua. Gibeonites and other groups of Canaanites were not expelled, however. They became "hewers of wood and drawers of water" (Joshua 9:21, 23, 27).

b. Shem is blessed: "Blessed be the Lord God of Shem." Shem's blessing is in his knowledge of *Yahweh*, his God, and the God who is the creator of all things. Through Shem's line, in the fulness of time, the Savior appeared. Our word Semite (or Shemite) is used of the descendants of Shem. In modern usage it is applied to those who speak one of the languages termed Semitic.

c. Japheth is blessed, also, although his blessings are not of the spiritual quality which characterizes those of Shem. The progenitor of the Indo-European, or Aryan peoples, Japheth was given the promise of prosperity and political dominion. He dwells, however, "in the tents of Shem," enjoying the spiritual blessing of the Semite.

4. Noah's Death (9:28-29). No details are given concerning the 350 years of Noah's life after the flood except for the episode of his drunkenness and its aftermath. The 950 years of Noah's life compare favorably with the longevity of the ante-diluvians mentioned in chapter five.

34

I. (10:1-32) The Nations: Descendants of Noah.

The Bible clearly teaches the unity of the human race. As all men trace their origin to Adam, so all nations are descended from the sons of Noah. In whatsoever way *Yahweh* was identified as the God of Israel, the orthodox mind never lost sight of the fact that all nations and peoples sprang from common origins, and that *Yahweh* was the creator of all. When specialized blessings are pronounced on Abraham and his descendants, the other nations are not forgotten. Israel was to be a means of blessing to others. At the time of the call of Abraham, God declared, "In thee shall all the families of the earth be blessed" (12:3).

Like other Biblical genealogical tables, those presented here are selective. Seventy names are chosen. Some of these are well known to students of the Bible and ancient history (e.g. Mizraim — Egypt). Others are not identifiable in the present state of our knowledge. Some people, like the Sumerians, well known to historians, are not mentioned in the list. Sumerian cities, however, do appear. In some cases it is clear that peoples rather than individuals are meant. The *-im* ending is the Hebrew plural.

1. The Sons of Japheth (10:1-5). Among the Japhethites whose identification seems positive are:

Madai — The Medes.

Javan — The Ionians, or Greeks.

Kittim — The Cypriotes, from Cyprus.

Dodanim (I Chronicles 1:7 reads "Rodanim") — Inhabitants of the Island of Rhodes and neighboring Aegean islands.

2. The Sons of Ham (10:6-20). Although the center of Hamite culture appears to be in northern Africa, they spread early in various directions as is evident from the peoples named. These include:

Cush — Ethiopians.

Mizraim — Egypt ("Mizraim" became the common Hebrew name for Egypt).

Put — Identified by inscriptions of Darius I as Put(a) in Cyrenaica. Earlier thought to be Punt, or Somaliland.

Canaan — The Canaanites.

Sheba — Southern Arabians (cf. "The Queen of Sheba").

Babel, Erech, Accad — Cities in southern Mesopotamia.

Nineveh — Became Assyrian capital.

Philistines — Gave their name to Palestine.

Zidon — Canaanite (Phoenician) city.

Heth — Progenitor of the Hittites.

Jebusites — Canaanites who dwelt in Jerusalem (Jebus) before David's conquest.

Arvadites and Hamathites — Inhabitants of Phoenician cities of Arvad and Hamath.

The significant individual here mentioned is Nimrod, whose kingdom centered at Babel and reached to Assyria where he built several cities, including Nineveh. Note the Revised Standard Version of verse 11, "He went into Assyria," which is preferable to the King James Version, "Out of that land went forth Asshur."

Nimrod is described as being "a mighty hunter before the Lord" (10:9). Assyrian art frequently depicts hunting scenes, and gives evidence that Assyrian monarchs were frequently fond of the chase. The proverbial hunter, Nimrod, achieved political power extending his dominion over Babel, Erech, Accad, Calneh, and other cities in the Tigris-Euphrates valley.

3. The Sons of Shem (10:21-31). The genealogy of Shem is placed last because of its relation to what follows. Most of Bible history centers around the descendants of Shem. The names include:

Elam — The Elamites or Persians.

Asshur — The Assyrians.

Lud — The Lydians of Asia Minor.

Aram — The Arameans, or Syrians.

Eber — The Hebrews. Through Abraham, Eber is the father of the Hebrew people. Abraham is called *Ha-ibri*, "the Hebrew" (14:13). The term is frequently used by foreign peoples in referring to Israelites.

J. (11:1-9) The Tower of Babel.

In the reference to Peleg (10:25) it is stated that "in his days was the earth divided." It has been thought that this is an allusion to the division of the peoples at Babel. The division of the world into various peoples, described in chapter 10, was a natural process. Chapter eleven presents an unnatural dispersion as a result of divine judgment. Whatever development there was in language before the flood, Noah and his family preserved but one tongue. The subsequent development of various languages is traced to an act of divine judgment.

1. The Building of the Tower (11:1-4). The purpose of the building of the tower is described as two-fold:

a. Positive: "Let us make us a name." This is the sin of pride and self-sufficiency. God is, by inference, repudiated.

b. Negative: "Lest we be scattered." They desired the strength which comes from unity. It was unity without God, however.

The materials of the tower, brick and slime, are the building materials of lower Babylon where there is no natural stone.

The description of the tower, "with its top in heaven" (11:4) may be regarded as an hyperbole (cf. Deuteronomy 1:28). Yet the entire narrative breathes the air of defiance against the God of heaven.

2. The Judgment of God (11:5-9). The judgment of God had two results:

a. Their tongues were confounded.

Linguistic unity had furthered the rebellious plans of the dwellers of Babel. This unity was broken, not to reappear until Pentecost when "the multitude came together and were confounded because that every man heard them (the apostles) speak in his own language" (Acts 2:6).

There is no hint that language and race are in any way connected. In modern terminology, a Semite is one who speaks a Semitic language. Such terminology has the virtue of convenience, but it cannot be considered to be scientifically accurate.

The confusion of tongues at Babel does not imply that the languages assumed a fixed form then and have remained unchanged ever since. Every language and dialect has a complicated history, and every living language is subject to continual change.

b. The people were scattered.

The act of rebellion brought about the very thing which the inhabitants of Babel wished to prevent. The Bible emphasizes the unity of the race in Adam and Noah, and its division which is accounted for, in part, by the arrogant pride of self-satisfied man.

The name of Babel meant, to the Babylonians themselves, "the gate of God." To the Hebrews it was associated with the Hebrew root *bll* (11:9) so that, by a play on words, it came to mean "confusion."

Whatever became of the Tower of Babel? North of the Temple of Marduk in Babylon is a temple-tower, or ziggurat, known as Etemenanki, "The House of the Terrace-platform of Heaven and Earth." It is possible that the unfinished Tower of Babel was put to use in the building of this ziggurat which dominated the sky line of Babylon in a later day.

K. (11:10-26) Shem's Descendants through Terah.

Terah appears as the tenth name in the genealogy of Shem as Noah was the tenth from Adam. There are omissions, however. Names are included in 10:21-25 which do not appear here.

Eber, from whom the name "Hebrew" is derived (cf. under 10:21) possibly means "immigrant" or "one who passes over." Salah may have given it to his son on the occasion of some tribal movement. It is also possible that the word is a derogatory one, signifying a trespasser. In this sense it would be a word coined by the settled communities to describe the loosely organized bands which threatened them. Cuneiform literature abounds with references to such a people known as *ḥa-BI-ru*. It is clear, however, that the *ḥa-BI-ru* cannot be equated with the Biblical Hebrews. Some of the cuneiform references antedate Abraham. The most that can be said is that the descendants of Abraham may have been termed *ḥa-BI-ru* by some with whom they came in contact. Meredith Klein (*Westminster Theological Journal*, XIX, 1, 2, and XX, 1), maintains that the *ḥa-BI-ru* were actually foes of Israel.

L. (11:27-32) Terah and His Family.

Ur, the home of Terah, has been identified by most writers with Al-Muqayyar, a town on the Euphrates some distance east of its junction with the Tigris in lower Mesopotamia. Excavations by C. Leonard Wooley, director of the Joint Expedition of the British Museum and the University of Pennsylvania Museum, have demonstrated the high level of the culture of Ur during the years before Abraham. Its jewelry and art are unsurpassed.

The theory of a northern Ur, northeast of Haran, has recently been revived by Cyrus H. Gordon ("Abraham and the Merchants of Ura" in *Journal of Near Eastern Studies*, XVII, 1). Dr. Gordon notes the existence of a warlike people known as the Chaldeans who blocked the way to Armenia, described in the *Anabasis* v. 5. 17. Similarly Isaiah 23:13 refers to a Land of the Chaldeans which appears to have a northern locale. Tablets describing the foreign trade of merchants from a northern city of Ura lead Dr. Gordon to suggest that Abraham's city was in the northern area, rather than at al-Muqayyar.

From Ur, Terah and his family migrated to Haran, an important commercial city about 280 miles northeast of Damascus. Abram left Haran for Canaan when his father was 145 years of age. Terah lived another sixty years in Haran before he died at the age of 205 (compare 11:26 with 12:4). In Acts 7:4, however, Stephen states that Abraham left Haran "when his father was dead."

This apparent contradiction has puzzled Bible students. Some have suggested that the order of Terah's sons (11:26) is not chronological, and that Abram is placed first because of his prominence. This is a plausible suggestion and, if correct, we would have no means of dating the years of Abram with reference to Terah's life span. Others, however, suggest that the record of Terah's death in Genesis 11:32 reflects the desire of the inspired historian to conclude his reference to Terah at this point, inasmuch as the importance of Terah "is absorbed in his being the father of Abram" (Delitzsch). Stephen's address, then, would refer to the order of events recorded in Genesis 11 and 12 rather than the chronology of those events.

II The History of the Patriarch (Chaps. 12-50)

The opening chapters of Genesis dealt with the entire human race. Adam is presented as the progenitor of all mankind, not simply of Israel. The sin of Adam is imputed to all, so that Gentile as well as Jew stands guilty before God. These facts are basic to Paul's teaching concerning the redemptive work of Christ (cf. Romans 3:9ff., I Corinthians 15:22).

The greater part of Genesis, however, describes God's dealings with Abraham and his "seed," or the people of Israel. Four great characters, known as the fathers, or "patriarchs" are presented in these chapters: Abraham, Isaac, Jacob, and Joseph. The promises of God were made to, and received by, Abraham. Although he had other sons, Isaac was the one through whom these promises were to be realized (cf. 21:12). Similarly Jacob, although not the older son, received (by trickery, to be sure) the blessing of Isaac and became heir (27:27-29). The children of Jacob, or Israel, are all of significance in the development of God's purposes, however. Although Joseph occupies the prime position in the latter part of Genesis, it is clear that the tribes are to function as a unit. God's covenant at Sinai was made with all of the tribes, all received the law and, under Joshua, each received an inheritance in the land of Canaan. Levi became the tribe to which priestly responsibilities were assigned. David and his dynasty of kings came from the tribe of Judah. The sons of Joseph, Ephraim, and Manasseh, each received a tribal inheritance so that later history does not speak of a tribe of Joseph.

A. (12:1—25:18) The Patriarch Abraham.

We know nothing of the life of Abram (later, Abraham) in Ur of the Chaldees except for the fact that there he married Sarai (later, Sarah). Acts 7:2 states that God's first call came to Abram in Ur "before he came to Haran." The Genesis account does not mention this fact. It is in full accord, however, with the information presented in Genesis. Joshua 24:2 states that the ancestors of Israel in Ur "served other gods." An interesting Jewish tradition makes Terah an idol-maker by trade. The moon god was the principle deity of Haran and the surrounding area, and it is likely that Terah and his family were devotees of

Sin (the Semitic name for the Sumerian Nannar, the Moon god). The call to leave Ur of the Chaldees evidently included both Terah and Abram.

1. The Call of Abram (12:1-9). Abram journeyed from Ur to Haran with his father Terah. There, after an undisclosed length of time, he again heard the voice of the Lord and departed for Canaan with Sarai his wife, his nephew Lot, and "the souls that they had gotten in Haran." The latter probably refers to the slaves and their dependants which were a part of Abram's household. Rabbinical commentators interpreted the "souls" as proselytes won by Abram and Sarai during their sojourn at Haran.

God's promise to Abram included not only prosperity and blessing for his descendants, but also an outreach that is worldwide in scope: "In thee shall all the families of the earth be blessed" (12:3b). Many modern translators render the Niphal form (nivreku): "bless themselves" instead of "be blessed." While the reflexive sense is possible, the passive is to be preferred. The Jewish Publication Version (1917) translates the form as passive, but the Revised Standard Version has taken the reflexive sense.

It is clear, whichever translation is preferred, that God called Abram from polytheistic Ur and Haran to be a witness to Himself. Through Abram's line the Messiah would come. The Scriptures, the "Oracles of God," came first to the prophets of Israel. Yet, in the very beginning of Israel's history, God reminded Abram that his blessings were a means to a greater end. Through Abram, blessing would reach all the earth. While the call of Abram marks a transition from universal to particular history, the reminder is given at the very beginning of Israel's history that the scope of God's concern, and, ultimately, of His promises, was universal.

Entering Canaan, Abram first settled in the sparsely populated area around Shechem in the hills of what was to become Samaria. Later he "pitched his tent" between Bethel and Ai. Abram and his immediate descendants lived a semi-nomadic life, moving from place to place with their flocks. Necessary pasturage, and wells to supply water, would determine the place of temporary settlement.

Although Abram's wealth was never measured by holdings in real estate, the future possession of Canaan was promised to his family. The Canaanite was not dispossessed until the time of Joshua, yet Abram had the promise: "Unto thy seed will I give this land" (12:7).

2. Abram in Egypt (12:10-20). After spending some time in the dry Negeb, or south country, Abram was forced by famine to seek a place of fertility in Egypt. Egypt borders the Negeb, so that the journey would not be a long one. The rains of Palestine are necessary for fruitful seasons, but Egypt is irrigated by the annual overflow of the Nile. In times of famine, the inhabitant of Canaan first thought of Egypt as the place to go for food. There is no hint that Abram did wrong in going to Egypt at this time, but his conduct there was certainly both cowardly and evil.

The lie by which Abram attempted to fool Pharaoh and spare himself at Sarai's expense cannot be condoned. The attempt to "do evil that good may come" inevitably leads to tragedy.

The Egyptian tale known as the *Story of the Two Brothers* tells of a pharaoh who insisted on having a Palestinian maiden brought to him after he smelled a lock of her hair. The pharaohs ruled as gods and their every whim was respected. Abram's fear was probably well founded, but his lack of courage and trust in God were unworthy of a man of faith.

Pharaoh's attitude upon learning the truth about Sarai's relationship to Abram is commendable. Sarai was restored to her husband, but they were then ushered out of Egypt in disgrace.

3. The Parting of Abram and Lot (13:1-18).

a. Abram at Bethel (13:1-4). Leaving Egypt, Abram entered the Negeb and moved northward toward Bethel, where he had earlier built an altar. The experiences in Egypt doubtless impelled Abram to renew the vows which he had previously made at Bethel.

b. The Problem of Prosperity (13:5-13). Both Abram and Lot lived nomadic lives. Their wealth was in their herds and flocks. With the passing of the years they prospered to the point where their herdsmen quarreled over pasturage. The presence of Canaanites, Perizites, and other natives of Palestine further reduced the amount of available ground. The bickering of the herdsmen was not only a source of contention; it was a poor testimony to those who had heard from Abram concerning the nature of his God. Abram determined to remove the cause of contention by suggesting that Lot separate from him, taking his choice of the available land. Lot chose the plain, or "circle" of the Jordan, an exceptionally fertile area which included Sodom and Gomorrah at the southern tip of the Dead Sea.

From the standpoint of material prosperity, Lot's choice seemed wise. It included fertile fields and large and prosperous cities. The wickedness of the area, however, should have deterred Lot from becoming too closely allied with it.

Abram willingly accepted the less desirable land to the west, in Canaan. A. P. Stanley says of Lot, "He chose the rich soil, and with it the corrupt civilization which had grown up in the rank climate of that deep descent; and left to Abraham the hardships, the glory, and the virtue of the rugged hills, the sea-breezes, and the inexhaustible future of Western Palestine."

c. The Promise to Abram (13:14-18). Grieved at the departure of Lot, and conscious of the fact that the best of the land was no longer available to him, Abram was in need of the encouragement which he received.

God promised to Abram the land of Canaan, which he could view in all directions, and a posterity which would be innumerable like the dust of the earth. Abram moved to the area of Hebron which evidently belonged to an Amorite named Mamre (cf. 14:13). The heir of the divine promises still dwelt in tents. It is significant that at each new settlement of the patriarchs we read of the building of an altar. The worship of God was particularly appropriate after having received the renewal of the divine promises.

4. The Battle of the Kings (14:1-24). In the period following the establishment of the monarchy, the Bible records many instances of the relations between the nation of Israel and her neighbors. Secular documents add to our knowledge of Biblical times by describing battles in which the Israelites participated. Kings of Israel (e.g. Jehu and Hezekiah) are mentioned in cuneiform inscriptions, and a wealth of material is available to describe the exploits of a Sennacherib, Nebuchadnezzar, or Cyrus.

Before the establishment of the United Kingdom (c. 1000 B.C.), Israel was not thought of as a world power. The history of Abraham's descendants begins as the history of a family. At the time of the exodus from Egypt it is the history of a federation of twelve tribes, having common family origins.

In the simple, patriarchal life of the fathers of Israel, contacts with world powers were at the personal or tribal level. Genesis 14, however, gives us a picture of political and military life in

Abraham's day. Sacred history includes these episodes because Lot, Abraham's nephew, became involved in the political life of Sodom.

a. Rebellion and Reprisals (14:1-13). The kings of the city-states at the southern tip of the Dead Sea were subdued by a confederacy of eastern kings, who forced them to pay annual tribute. This area, now barren, was fruitful and prosperous before the cataclysm which destroyed Sodom and Gomorrah and the "cities of the plain." Archaeologists have noted a definite change in the area about 2000 B.C.

After paying tribute for twelve years, Sodom and her allies decided to refuse payment. This was interpreted as active rebellion. The following year (the fourteenth after tribute had been first imposed) the eastern confederacy sent a punitive expedition which brought complete defeat to the cities of the Dead Sea area.

The names of the eastern kings cannot be identified with other historical rulers, but similar names do occur in the cuneiform literature. Amraphel has been equated with Hammurabi, the Babylonian lawgiver, but chronological considerations argue against the identification. Arioch, king of Ellasar, would probably read "Eriaku, king of Larsa," in a contemporary Sumerian document. Chedorlaomer would be rendered "Kudur-Lagamar" — servant of Lagamar, an Elamite deity. Tidal would probably be "Tudghula." He is described as "king of nations" (goyim). Either he ruled a confederacy of nations, or goyim is a Hebrew rendering of Gutium. A similar name is borne by one of the Hittite kings.

The eastern confederacy apparently advanced from the Damascus area, moving through Bashan and the Amorite territory east of the Jordan to a point south of the Dead Sea. They then turned northward by way of Hazezon-tamar (possibly Engedi), fighting the leaders of the revolt in the Vale of Siddim, near Sodom and Gomorrah.

The peoples mentioned in verse five — Rephaim, Zuzim, and Emim — were aboriginal inhabitants of the area afterward occupied by Edom, Moab, and Ammon. Once thought of as mythological, the Rephaim are now identified in the Ugaritic texts as a historical people. The Horites (verse 6) are now well-known as Hurrians, whose settlement at Nuzu has yielded clay tablets which illustrate many of the patriarchal customs. The Eastern confederacy had no difficulty in defeating all of these peoples.

The kings of Sodom and Gomorrah, with their allies, seem to have planned on using the Vale of Siddim as a kind of natural defense. The slimepits of the area were holes from which bitumen had been excavated. Expecting to use this terrain to confound the enemy, the kings of the area suffered a decisive defeat there. The Eastern confederacy took whatever they wished as booty and departed. The booty included slaves. The fact that Lot was among those taken brings this bit of history into the Biblical record.

b. The Rescue of Lot (14:14-17). The episode of the capture of Lot was reported to "Abram the Hebrew," who immediately organized a rescue party. This is the first mention of the word "Hebrew" in the Bible. It appears to be derived from Eber (cf. 10:21, 11:14) and usually occurs in contexts where Abram or his descendants are being identified before foreigners. A people known as the Habiru or Apiru is mentioned in the cuneiform literature of Tell-el-Amarna in Egypt, Nuzu, and Mari in Mesopotamia. It seems clear that the Hebrews of the Bible are not to be identified with these Habiru, but it is possible that they shared the name and reputation with other groups. The Habiru of the cuneiform tablets were trouble-makers on the fringes of society who were disturbing the settled communities. The term may have come to mean "semi-nomads" which would, of course, describe the patriarchs and their families.

The fact that Abram could assemble 318 armed servants at a moment's notice is evidence of his wealth. The Beni Hassan tomb painting, showing a group of Semites entering Egypt about 1900 B.C., gives evidence of the high culture of the Palestinian nomad. The men wear short skirts and sandals, the women, shoes and long dresses fastened by a single shoulder-clasp. Weapons include a spear, bow, and throw-stick. One man has a skin water-bottle on his back and a lyre (Biblical "harp") in his hands. The woolen clothes are variegated in color.

Cyrus H. Gordon has shown (*Journal of Near Eastern Studies,* XVII, 1: "Abraham and the Merchants of Ura") that the patriarchs were much more than Bedouin nomads. Abraham was a trader, rich in silver and gold as well as cattle (cf. Genesis 20:16). He had armed servants who would normally be employed to protect his flocks and other possessions.

In the emergency of Lot's capture, Abram asked the help of his allies, Aner, Eshcol, and Mamre. They marched northward to Dan, and defeated the Eastern confederacy there in a surprise attack. Dan may best be regarded as a modernization of the

46

name Laish, which would have been used before the conquest of the ancient city by the Danites (Joshua 19:47; Judges 18:29). The Second Book of Samuel 24:6 mentions a Dan-Jaan which some have located in Gilead (cf. Deuteronomy 34:1). The Septuagint and the Vulgate render Dan-Jaan as "Dan in the Woods."

The magnitude of the undertaking is shown both by the size of Abram's private army and the ground they traversed. After defeating the enemy at Dan, Abram pursued them to Hobah, north of Damascus. He recovered all of the booty which they had taken, including Lot.

c. Abram and Melchizedek (14:18-20). Abram, after receiving the thanks of the king of Sodom for his services in defeating the Eastern confederacy, received a blessing from Melchizedek ("King of Righteousness") the king of Salem (Jerusalem). The name "Salem" means "peace." Jerusalem occurs in the Amarna tablets as *Urusalim*. It probably signifies the "foundation of Shalem" or "city of Shalem." Shalem was the Canaanite god of peace, and pre-Israelite Jerusalem may have been devoted to his worship. The name of Jerusalem does not occur in the Pentateuch, but it is used nine times in Joshua. It was settled by the Jebusites and called Jebus until captured by the Israelites under David (Joshua 15:8; Judges 19:10; II Samuel 5:8).

The names of Jebus and *Urusalim* may both have been used during the pre-Israelite occupation of Jerusalem. It had the latter name during the nineteenth century B.C., as shown in Egyptian texts which speak of *Urusalimum*. In Biblical usage any relationship to a Canaanite deity is rejected. Jerusalem is the city of peace, and Melchizedek is king of the city-state of Salem, or peace.

The word "priest" first appears in Scripture in the account of Melchizedek. The patriarchs offered their own sacrifices, performing the function of priests in their own households. In the Mosaic legislation, the tribe of Levi and the house of Aaron were set apart for priestly ministry. It is significant that pre-Mosaic Melchizedek was both priest and king, whereas the two offices were carefully separated in subsequent Israelite history. The tribe of Judah and the line of David yielded the legitimate kings. In Psalm 110 and Hebrews 7 the royal priesthood of Melchizedek is seen as a prefigurement of the Messianic priesthood. Christ, like Melchizedek, is a priest-king.

47

Melchizedek was one of the few Semites who had not fallen into idolatry before Abram's call. Abram identified the God of Melchizedek (*'El 'Elyon,* "God most high") with *Yahweh,* the God whom he served. The name *'El 'Elyon* is common in the religious documents of Ras-Shamra — Ugarit (14th century B.C.).

The bread and wine which Melchizedek brought to Abram (14:18) were tokens of friendship and hospitality. We are also told that Melchizedek blessed Abram. As a priest, Melchizedek ranked above Abram, for "the less is blessed of the greater" (Hebrews 7:7). Abram's payment of tithes was a further recognition of Melchizedek's priesthood. The author of the epistle to the Hebrews, in showing the superiority of Christ to the Aaronic priesthood, states that Jesus was not a priest of the order of Aaron. He was priest of an order more ancient than that of Aaron, that of Melchizedek, whom Abram recognized as priest of God Most High.

d. Abram and the King of Sodom (14:21-24). The king of Sodom recognized his debt to Abram. The victor in battle had the legal right to keep the spoils of war. He was expected to restore the people who had been taken captive, but the property was his to keep. The king of Sodom suggested that Abram accept the "goods" but he declined. The allies, Aner, Eshcol, and Mamre, were to receive their due, but Abram insisted that he would take nothing for himself. He recognized that his riches were a trust from God. He felt that it would dishonor God for him to accept wealth from the king of Sodom.

5. The Promise of an Heir (15:1-21). In his dealings with the king of Sodom, Abram showed himself to be a faithful child of God. Yet Abram carried a great burden. God had made certain promises to Abram which would be fulfilled through his "seed." Abram had reached old age and he was still without an heir.

a. Abram's Fear (15:1-3). God, mindful of Abram's doubts and fears, declared, "Fear not, Abram, I am thy shield and thy exceeding great reward." If this translation is correct, God declared Himself to be the defense to Abram in time of trouble and the reward to Abram in lieu of worldly gain. Most modern translations follow the Septuagint in reading, "I am thy shield and thy reward is exceeding great." Since the Hebrew text can be read either way, it is impossible to insist on one translation as definitive. The words "thy reward is exceeding great," are in complete accord with the context, for Abram immediately objected that God's promise was meaningless. God's promises required an heir, and Abram's legal heir was a servant named Eliezer.

Abram had evidently conformed to local custom and adopted a trusted servant. The Nuzu tablets of the fifteenth and fourteenth centuries B.C. contain many examples of such adoptions. They show us that an adopted son remains heir unless a natural son is subsequently born. A natural son takes precedence over an adopted son, although the latter has certain legal rights which must be recognized.

b. God's Response (15:4-5). God assured Abram that a natural born son would become his heir. God further instructed Abram to look toward the heavens and count the stars. His seed would be as beyond computation as the stars of the heavens. God had declared the impossible, for Abram was past the time of life when he could hope to become a father.

c. Abram's Faith (15:6). Abram knew that it was humanly impossible for him to beget a child in his old age, but he believed, or trusted God. Both reason and human experience would argue the impossibility of the birth of a child to Abram and Sarai. By believing God, Abram became the "father" of the faithful of all ages, whatever their physical lineage (cf. Romans 4:3, 19-23).

In Egypt, Abram had showed a lack of faith by denying his wife before Pharaoh. Now, Abram is reckoned righteous on the basis of his faith. By believing God in the matter of an heir, he gives evidence of trust in all that God has revealed. Abram's justification by faith is cited in the New Testament as an evidence of the way in which God justifies the sinner (Romans 4:3; Galatians 3:6). As a man of faith, Abram believed that God would one day send the Savior (cf. John 8:56). On the basis of this faith, Abram was justified.

d. The Solemn Covenant (15:7-17). Ancient covenants were frequently confirmed by cutting a sacrificial victim in half. The two parties to the covenant then passed between the portions of the slain animal. In this way the parties to the covenant were symbolically united by the bond of common blood. God condescended to confirm his covenant with Abram in accord with this custom.

After Abram had prepared the sacrificial victims, in accord with God's directions, "the birds of prey came down upon the carcasses." They served to foreshadow the obstacles which Abram's seed would experience before entering into their possessions.

At this solemn moment God unveiled the future of Abram's descendants to the aged patriarch. Abram's seed would be afflicted four hundred years in a "strange" land (Egypt), after which they would return to inherit the land which had been promised to Abram. Although these promises could not be realized in Abram's lifetime, he was promised a long and full life (verse 15). Not only is the material aspect of the promises to Abraham frequently stressed, but it is also clear that he was a man of spiritual vision. The Epistle to the Hebrews says, "He looked for a city which hath foundations, whose builder and maker is God" (11:10).

A "flaming torch" passed between the pieces of the sacrifice at the time when the sun was setting. Unlike covenants between equals, God alone assumed responsibility in His covenant with Abram. God may be thought of as having made promises to Abram in the form of a covenant (cf. Galatians 3:16-18).

The reason for God's delay in giving the land to Abram is instructive. God is both just and patient. The descendants of Abram would one day inhabit the land of Canaan. The earlier inhabitants of the land would be dispossessed because of their sin. Yet God was patient. The iniquity of the Amorite was not yet full (verse 16). God is not arbitrary in His dealings with any group of men. Full opportunity was given for the Amorite to repent and turn to God. Judgment was mercifully delayed. When God's mercy is spurned, however, judgment is sure.

e. The Extent of the Promise (15:18-21). The area promised as the ultimate possession of Abram's seed included the territory from the northern reaches of the Euphrates to the land of Egypt. Scholars differ as to whether the *nehar Mitzraim* ("river of Egypt") mentioned here is to be equated with the *naḥal Mitzraim* ("brook of Egypt"), or with the Nile as the "River of Egypt." The *naḥal Mitzraim* is often mentioned, both in Biblical and secular sources, as the southern boundary of Palestine. It is known by its Arabic name, *Wady el Arish*. However interpreted, it is clear that the land of promise included the area from Syria to Egypt. Egypt itself was not included. It was "a land not theirs" (verse 13). The western boundary of the promised land was the Mediterranean, and the Jordan River served as the eastern boundary. Two and one-half tribes settled east of the Jordan in Joshua's day, but this was by special permission. The east-Jordan territory did not form a part of the land promised to Abram.

The borders here described were actually reached twice in the history of Israel. At the dedication of Solomon's Temple we read of an assemblage of Israelites "from the entrance of Hamath to the Brook of Egypt" (I Kings 8:65). Of Jeroboam II it is written, "He restored the border of Israel from the entrance of Hamath unto the Sea of the Arabah" (i.e. the Dead Sea). Due to disobedience, Israel's boundaries were much narrower at other times.

6. The Birth of Ishmael (16:1-16). Abram had been concerned lest his servant Eliezer become his heir (15:1-2). God responded by a solemn promise that Abram's heir would be his own flesh and blood (15:4). Years passed, however, and no son was born. Abram and Sarai were perplexed, and perhaps a bit impatient.

a. Sarai's Suggestion (16:1-3). Calvin observes, "The faith of Abram and Sarah was defective; not, indeed, with regard to the substance of the promise; but with regard to the method in which they proceeded." According to the Biblical ideal of monogamy (cf. Genesis 2:24), Sarai's offer of her handmaid as a secondary wife for Abram was wrong and sinful. Her conduct, however, has ample precedent in the cuneiform records of the ancient Near East. The purpose of marriage was not companionship but procreation. Marriage contracts among the Nuzu tablets explicitly state that it is the responsibility of the wife to bear children. If she does not do so, she is obligated to provide an handmaid, as Sarai did. Sarai was acting in full accord with the customs of her day, although the solution to the problem of her inability to bear a child was not acceptable to God. In our society her suggestion would be unthinkable, but in hers it was normal, acceptable procedure.

b. Contention between Hagar and Sarai (16:4-6). After Hagar conceived, Sarai fancied that she observed disrespectful behavior on the part of her maid. Hagar's relation to Abram did not alter her status as Sarai's handmaid. Sarai insisted that Abram intervene to right the real or fancied wrongs which had developed as a result of her own suggestion.

The Nuzu tablets mention the relationship between the wife and the handmaid in such cases. The servile status of the handmaid is not altered by her giving birth to a child. In the event of a subsequent birth by the wife, certain rights of the handmaid are specified. Neither she nor her child are to be dismissed from the household.

c. Hagar's Flight (16:7-8). When Abram learned of the difficulties between his wife and Hagar, he suggested that Sarai do as she saw fit in the matter. Fearing humiliation or punishment, Hagar fled toward the land of Egypt, doubtless expecting to find a place of refuge in her homeland. She was on her way to Shur when she stopped by a fountain to rest. Shur means "wall." The Egyptians maintained a line of fortresses on their eastern frontier to protect their land from Asiatic nomads. The wall of Egypt is mentioned in records of the Twelfth Dynasty (c. 2000-1775 B.C.). The land to the east of the wall was known as the Wilderness of Shur — the wilderness area outside the wall of Egypt.

d. The Message of the Angel (16:8-12). At a spring, in the wilderness, on the way to Shur, the Angel of the Lord met Hagar. This is the first appearance in Scripture of the term *Mal 'ak Yahweh,* the Angel of the Lord. This being appears to partake of the nature of *Yahweh,* Himself. Davis in his *Bible Dictionary,* notes: "The Angel of the Lord thus appears as a manifestation of Jehovah Himself, one with Jehovah and yet different from Him." While this cannot be regarded as a clear teaching of the triune nature of the God of Israel, it does indicate a "richness within the unity of the Godhead" (Kevan) which serves as a preparation for the fuller revelation of God in the New Testament.

The Angel of the Lord met Hagar at a time when Hagar needed help. At a spring in the desert Hagar heard a command which would seem humiliating and distasteful: "Return to thy mistress and submit thyself to her hand."

The promise included both immediate and remote factors. Hagar was consoled by the promise that her seed would be multiplied to the point where it could not be counted. In the more immediate future Hagar would bear a son to be named Ishmael ("God heareth"). He will be a typical son of the desert, resisting the encroachments of civilization and maintaining a position of independence before his brethren. The term "wild ass of a man" is not an insult, but rather a metaphor based on the free and roving character of the wild ass.

e. The Response of Hagar (16:13-16). Hagar's response was one of faith. She identified the "Angel" who had spoken to her with the "God of Seeing" — the God who had seen her and ministered to her in her distress. He is also the God who manifests Himself so that the needy may, with the eye of faith, see Him. The well where Hagar stopped for refreshment was named, "The Well of the Living One that Seeth Me."

A child was born as the Angel had prophesied. Abram concurred in giving him the name of Ishmael. At the time of the birth of Ishmael, Abram had reached the age of eighty-six.

7. The Covenant with Abraham (17:1-27). The initiative of Sarai and Abram in attempting to accomplish God's purposes through Hagar had produced difficulties instead of solutions to their problem. God again intervened to assure Abram that his heir would be neither Eliezer nor Ishmael but a son of his wife, Sarai. The covenant established in 15:18 is thus renewed.

a. The Theophany (17:1). *Yahweh* appeared to Abram, identifying Himself as *'El Shaddai*, "God Almighty." The derivation of *Shaddai* is uncertain. "Almighty" is the translation used in the Latin Vulgate, and appears to be the force of the word. Others derive it from a root meaning "to heap benefits," suggesting that God here identifies Himself as the Friend who shepherds the patriarchs and preserves them from all harm. The word has also been equated, unsatisfactorily, with a Semitic word for mountain.

b. The Promise (17:2-8). At critical moments in Abram's life God repeated and supplemented the promises which had earlier been given (cf. 12:2-3; 12:7; 13:14-17; 15:5-6). God's patience with Abram is evident at each episode.

God here specifies a personal relationship: He will be Abram's God. He will protect, bless, and multiply Abram and his posterity. Abram's name is changed. Ab-ram means "exalted father," whereas Ab-raham means "father of a multitude." The emphasis is on God's purposes for the future.

c. The Obligation (17:9-14). In addition to the general command, "Walk before me and be thou upright" (17:1), God enjoined the rite of circumcision as a sign or symbol of the covenant. Every male child was to be circumcised on the eighth day as a sign of his relationship to the God of Abraham. Circumcision was not an absolutely new rite. It had existed among many peoples of the ancient Fertile Crescent, including the Egyptians. The "uncircumcised Philistine" was an exception. The practice, however, was adopted as a sign of the covenant, at the direction of God.

d. The Son To Be Born to Sarah (17:15-22). The name of Sarai was changed to Sarah. The latter form of the name emphasizes the role which Sarah will play in history. As a "princess" she will be a mother of nations.

53

In his advanced age, Abraham was not prepared for this new revelation. Ishmael had become dear to him, and he was perfectly content to allow Ishmael to be his heir. God assured Abraham that Ishmael would be the father of a great people, but the specific line of covenant promise would be realized in a son of Sarah to be named Isaac.

e. The Obedience of Abraham (17:23-27). Abraham immediately accepted God's word and covenant. Ishmael and all the men of Abraham's household received the rite of circumcision in token of their relation to God's covenant. Although Ishmael's descendants do not form the line of promise, the blessings of the covenant are available to them. Ishmael is encouraged to hope for a share in the Messianic blessing.

8. The Destruction of Sodom and Gomorrah (18:1—19:38). Although our prime concern is with the promises to Abraham, the history of Lot is again introduced because of its relation to God's dealings with Abraham. It further shows the origin of the Moabites and the Ammonites, peoples with which Israel was to have much contact.

a. The Visit of the Angels (18:1-16). When Abraham, sitting at his tent door in the heat of the day, saw "three men," he urged them to accept his hospitality. This is the historical basis for the New Testament reminder, "Be not forgetful to entertain strangers, for thereby some have entertained angels unawares" (Hebrews 13:2).

The sense in which the visit of the angels is a theophany is not clear, but it may be assumed that the One designated as "The Angel of the Lord" was present. He doubtless was the one who asked the whereabouts of Sarah and gave the assurance that the following year she would give birth to a son.

Sarah laughed, thinking she was past the time of life when she could bear a son, but the Lord assured Abraham that a son would be born. The question, "Is anything too hard for the Lord?" may be compared with Luke 1:37: "For with God, nothing shall be impossible." The birth of Isaac required a miracle because his parents were past the time of life when they could naturally have children. The birth of Jesus was unique in that He was born of the Virgin Mary.

b. God's Revelation concerning Sodom (18:17-22). In view of the position which Abraham occupied in the divine purposes, God determined to reveal to him the destruction which was soon to overwhelm Sodom and the surrounding area. The destruction, like that of the flood, was not arbitrary, but part of God's moral government. Scripture does not teach that every catastrophe is related to specific sin, but it clearly indicates that all of history is subject to the control of God.

c. Abraham's Intercessory Prayer (18:23-33). In addition to the general concern for the welfare of his fellow human beings, Abraham had a particular concern for his nephew Lot. There is no hint of a change in Lot's attitude after his rescue from the Eastern confederacy (14). He still makes his home in Sodom and partakes of its life.

In his prayer, Abraham shows a high concept of the holiness and righteousness of God. He is convinced that "the God of all the earth" will "do justly." He reasons that the city should be spared for the sake of fifty righteous men who might be there. The Lord agrees, but it is obvious that fifty righteous men cannot be found in Sodom. Successively Abraham argues for the salvation of the city on the basis of 45, 40, 30, 20, and 10 righteous men. The Lord agrees, but there are not even ten righteous men in Sodom. Its destruction is imminent.

d. The Angels Rescue Lot (19:1-23). Lot, sitting at the gate of Sodom, observed two angels, appearing in the form of men, as they did to Abraham. He invited them into his house, as Abraham had invited them into his tent. The gate of an ancient oriental city served as a kind of "city hall." There all of the official business of the city was transacted. Professional scribes sat at the gate to write letters or prepare official documents. The men would congregate there to discuss the problems of the day (cf. Proverbs 31:23). Lot's presence at the gate implied an active participation in the life of Sodom. His "house" may be contrasted with the "tent" of Abraham. Abraham was a man of wealth, but all of his life was lived as a nomad. Lot became a city dweller.

The angelic visitors accepted Lot's offer of hospitality, but they were soon the objects of the sinful desires of the men of Sodom. To protect his visitors from molestation, Lot offered his own daughters to satisfy the lust of the Sodomites. The laws of hospitality demanded that guests be protected while under Lot's roof, whatever the personal cost to Lot and his loved ones. The men of Sodom were so depraved, however, that they were ready to pounce on Lot, when his guests rescued him and smote the Sodomites with a temporary blindness. The Hebrew text implies that the blindness was not permanent.

In this way Lot had a vivid illustration of the sin which was about to bring destruction on Sodom. The visitors warned Lot to prepare to leave Sodom. His daughters and sons-in-law were alerted, but the sons-in-law were typical men of Sodom, dismissing the warning as an idle tale. One of the tragedies of Lot's association with Sodom was the mixed marriages of his daughters.

Lot, his wife and daughters delayed until the last moment. Their guests had to practically drag them out of the city. When forced to leave, Lot pleaded for permission to flee to nearby Zoar. Lot never shared the depravity of the Sodomites. He is described as "righteous," but he was saved "as by fire."

e. The Destruction of Sodom (19:24-29). Lot and his family had no sooner left Sodom when judgment fell. God may have used an earthquake (cf. 19:21) as the means of the "overthrow" of the city and its environs. Compressed inflammable gases seem to have been set free. Becoming ignited, they rained down upon the area in fiery showers.

Lot's wife, looking back upon the burning city "became a pillar of salt." Her heart was in Sodom and she was judged with Sodom. "Her body became encrusted with a nitrous and saline substance that very likely preserved it from decay for some time" (DeSala). A similar fate befell lingering refugees at Pompeii.

f. Lot and His Family (19:30-38). With these verses the history of Lot is ended. No record has been preserved of his subsequent years. His sinful compromise with the men of Sodom bears fruit in the attitude of his daughters. Childless and widowed, they determine to have illicit relations with their father in order that they might bear children. Lot permitted himself to become intoxicated on two successive nights, in which condition the plans of his daughters were realized. Moab and Ben-ammi, the progenitors of the Moabites and the Ammonites, are thus accounted for. The story of Lot is a perennial warning against compromise. Lot, his wife, and his daughters all suffered. His sons-in-law, instead of being won by the example (as were the wives of Shem, Ham, and Japheth), lived and died as men of Sodom. Abraham's nephew had opportunities such as few have had, but his wasted life is a warning that opportunity brings responsibility.

9. Abraham and Abimelech of Gerar (20:1-18). The dealings of Abraham with Abimelech parallel those with Pharaoh (Genesis 12). As a matter of personal precaution he lied concerning his marital relation to Sarah.

a. Abimelech Takes Sarah (20:1-2). To protect himself in difficult situations Abraham made a habit of referring to Sarah as his "sister" (cf. 20:13). His Egyptian experience should have been a deterrant, but the Bible pictures honestly the lapses of its greatest characters.

b. God's Warning to Abimelech (20:3-7). God recognizes that Abimelech is innocent of any evil intent. Warned that Sarah is married to Abraham, Abimelech is obligated to restore her to her husband.

The term "prophet" is here used in the Bible for the first time. A prophet is a spokesman for God. Abraham, because of his special relation to God, is so designated, although the term is used more frequently of preacher-prophets like Elijah, Isaiah, and Jeremiah. The Hebrew canon of the Old Testament distinguishes the "former" or non-writing prophets — the books of Joshua, Judges, Samuel and Kings, from the "latter" or writing prophets — Isaiah, Jeremiah, Ezekiel and the twelve so-called minor prophets. Both Abraham and Moses, however, as spokesmen for God are termed prophets.

c. Abimelech Confronts Abraham (20:8-13). Abimelech properly rebuked Abraham for deceit. Abraham gave a lame excuse. He thought, "The fear of God is not in this place," i.e. "the people are so irreligious that they will not respect the sanctity of marriage." Sarah was actually a blood-relative, perhaps Terah's granddaughter. Semitic terms of relationship (son, daughter, brother, sister) are used to cover more remote as well as immediate relationships. Abraham's sin was in telling a half-truth, repressing the fact that she was also his wife.

d. Abimelech's Generosity and Blessing (20:14-18). Unlike Pharaoh, who expelled Abraham from Egypt upon the discovery of his deceit, Abimelech suggested that the patriarch settle wherever he wished in the area which he termed "my land." He also gave to Abraham a thousand pieces of silver as a "covering of the eyes." The words convey the idea of appeasement. Through the gift, the eyes of Abraham and any others involved would be blinded to the wrong done.

Abraham returned the kindness of Abimelech by prayer for God's blessing upon his household. Although both Abraham and Abimelech were at fault, the episode ends on a note of consideration and forgiveness.

10. Isaac and Ishmael (21:1-21).

a. The Birth of Isaac (21:1-7). In fulfillment of the divine promise, Sarah gave birth to a son, who received the name

Isaac ("laughter"). Mention was made of laughter in 17:17 and 18:12. Sarah had previously laughed in unbelief. Now she laughs in joy.

b. The Mockery of Isaac by Ishmael (21:8-10). At the feast celebrating the weaning of Isaac, Sarah was grieved when she observed Ishmael mocking her son. Ehrlich notes, "Ishmael laughed derisively at the feasting and rejoicing over the child Isaac, inasmuch as he was the elder son and the heir of his father's estate. Hence Sarah's natural desire to drive him out of the house."

Tablets from Nuzu, however, indicate that the son of a wife takes precedent over the son of an handmaid in the matter of inheritance. The succession of Abraham's heirs was: Eliezer, Ishmael, Isaac. With the birth of Isaac, Ishmael's position as heir to Abraham was replaced by Sarah's son.

c. The Expulsion of Hagar and Ishmael (21:11-22). Abraham was hesitant in the matter of the expulsion of Hagar and Ishmael. The Nuzu Tablets and the Code of Hammurabi indicate that the son of a bondwoman is not to be expelled after the birth of a son of a wife. God allayed the fears of Abraham, however, and indicated that Isaac was to be the child of promise: "In Isaac shall thy seed be called." Ishmael, however, was not forgotten. God assured Abraham that Ishmael would become a great nation, but the line of spiritual succession was that of Isaac.

Abraham's kindness is evident in the provision he made for Hagar and Ishmael. Departing from the patriarchal tent of Abraham, they sojourned in the area of Beer-sheba. Fearing death by starvation and thirst, Hagar wept, but God gave her reassurance concerning Ishmael's future and revealed a fountain of water which revived mother and son.

Ishmael was an adolescent at the time of Hagar's expulsion. This is evident from his action which caused Sarah's anger and from the indication of Abraham's age at the birth of Isaac. The Hebrew text does not imply that Ishmael was a babe in arms as does the King James Version (21:18).

The growth of Ishmael in the Wilderness of Paran, and the notice of his marrying an Egyptian girl indicate that he has reached maturity by this time.

11. Alliance between Abraham and Abimelech (21:22-33). Observing the blessing of God upon Abraham, Abimelech suggested an alliance of friendship which would be binding on Abimelech, Abraham, and their descendants. Abraham agreed,

but mentioned a grievance. Abimelech's servants had violently seized one of Abraham's wells. In nomadic life, wells are indispensable, and the absence of water compels the nomad to seek new pasture lands.

When Abimelech assured Abraham of ignorance concerning the episode, Abraham presented sheep and oxen as gifts designed to ratify the treaty. Seven ewe lambs were set aside as "witness" to the fact that Abraham had rights to the disputed well. For Abimelech to accept the lambs was to acknowledge this right.

The name Beer-sheba is given a double significance. *Shib 'ah* is the Hebrew word for "seven," and it is also the root of the verb "to swear" (Here is the form *nishb'u*, "they swore"). Beer-sheva or Beer-sheba is thus "the well of the seven" or "the well of the oath." Both ideas are implied in the word as described in verses 29-31.

After the departure of Abimelech, Abraham expressed his gratitude to God (*'El 'Ôlam*) under a tamarisk tree which he had planted. It is significant that *'El 'Ôlam* means "the eternal God," or "the everlasting God," a name particularly appropriate for use in connection with a covenant. Abraham was a creature of time, but his God was eternal.

12. The Offering of Isaac (22:1-19). Of the many tests which Abraham faced during his long life, that which involved the offering of his son, Isaac, was the most difficult and heart-rending. Abraham had received the promises of blessing through his "seed." The adopted son Eliezer, and the son of the handmaid, Ishmael were in turn replaced, and Isaac, the son of Abraham and Sarah became the child through whom God's promises would be realized.

a. The Test (22:1-2). Both absolute obedience and unquestioning trust in God are implied in the form in which Abraham's test is presented. To offer, as a sacrifice, the child through whom God's promises were to be realized, appears to be an irrational act. God seemed to be contradicting himself. Yet Abraham was required to obey God, regardless of his own reasoning in the matter. To see that God's promises would be realized even though Isaac be offered is a faith which trusts God's word regardless of the circumstances of life. Hebrews 11:17-19 states that Abraham believed that God would raise Isaac from the dead in order that the promises might be fulfilled.

b. The Obedience (22:3-10). Abraham's obedience was demonstrated in action rather than in words. He set out for the land of Moriah, as he had been directed, and prepared to sacrifice Isaac as a Burnt Offering. Abraham's statement to the servants that he and the lad would go, worship, and return is evidence that he "staggered not at the promise of God through unbelief."

Moriah is identified in II Chronicles 3:1 with the mountain on which Solomon built the Temple. It is now the site of the Moslem mosque known as the Dome of the Rock.

c. The Divine Provision (22:11-14). In the moment when the knife was raised to slay Isaac as a Burnt Offering, the Angel of the Lord intervened. Abraham was ordered not to harm Isaac, and a ram which had been caught in a thicket nearby was provided as a substitute sacrifice.

Child-sacrifice was common in Canaanite religion. Molech worship demanded the offering of humans, and such rites continued in days of apostasy down to the time of the destruction of Jerusalem by Nebuchadnezzar. In the beginning of the history of Abraham's family, however, God graphically repudiated child sacrifice, and its continuance was regarded as a deplorable "abomination." The depraved character of Canaanite religion resulted in the virtual expulsion of the Canaanites from their land in the days of Joshua (cf. Leviticus 18:2-3, 25; 20:2-5).

By divine command, Abraham spared Isaac. This fact seems to be in the mind of the apostle Paul when he writes: "He that spared not his own Son, but delivered him up for us all, how shall he not with him also freely give us all things?" (Romans 8:32).

Abraham named the place where he had prepared to sacrifice, "Jehovah-Jireh," literally, "The Lord ((*Yahweh*)) sees." With God, to see the need is to provide the remedy.

d. The Divine Blessing (22:15-19). The response of Abraham to the test to which he had been subjected was entirely satisfactory. He showed himself to be a man of faith and obedience. God, who could swear by none higher, swore by himself (i.e., affirmed on the integrity of His own name and reputation) that Abraham's "seed" would be as numerous as the sands of the seashore or the stars of the heaven. They would "possess the gate of their enemies," i.e. occupy the place of authority over those who would oppose them. The capture of the city gate meant the fall of the city itself.

It was God's purpose that through Abraham's "seed" blessing would come to "all the families of the earth." In its fullest sense this promise was to be fulfilled in the advent of Jesus. He was the "seed" *par excellence* (Galatians 3:16).

13. The Genealogy of Nahor (22:20-23). The line of Nahor was to be linked with that of Abraham in that Rebekah was to become the wife of Isaac (chapter 25). These verses thus form a part of the story of Abraham.

14. The Death and Burial of Sarah (23:1-20). Sarah's death at the age of 127 was a cause of sincere grief to Abraham. He was in the area of Kirjath Arba, or Hebron, at the time. Not owning any land, he proposed to purchase a burial plot from the Hittites who were dwelling in the area.

The Hittites suggested that he use burying places belonging to them, but Abraham insisted that he wished to purchase one of his own, suggesting the Cave of Machpelah which belonged to a Hittite named Ephron. Ephron did not wish to sell the cave, alone, but offered to "give" Abraham his field.

Studies in the Hittite Law Code, discovered at the ancient Hittite capital of Boghazkoy (in modern Turkey) indicate the reason for Ephron's desire to negotiate for the entire field. Certain feudal services were demanded of the owner of a piece of property. These obligations would be assumed by the new owner in the event of a transfer of property, unless the new owner acquired only a portion of the property. Abraham specified that he wished to purchase only the cave at the edge of the field (23:9) but Ephron insisted, "I sell you the field, and I sell you the cave which is in it" (23:11). He saw the possibility of ridding himself of his feudal obligations, and insisted that Abraham purchase the entire field.

The business transaction itself illustrates the commercial life of the period. Ephron, in politeness, offered the field as a gift. Abraham insisted on purchasing it. Casually Ephron suggested that a mere four hundred shekels of silver (his valuation on the land) should be esteemed as nothing — suggesting that Abraham bury his wife there without thought of recompense. In the Code of Hammurabi, six or eight shekels a year was the salary of a working man. Although Ephron's figure was exorbitant, Abraham "weighed out" the shekels (silver was not minted but weighed to determine its value). The description of the silver as "current money with the merchant" suggests a standard commercial grade of silver which had been legally established. The Code of Hammurabi mentions this practice in ancient commercial transactions. A kind of "Bureau of Weights and Measures" functioned, even in patriarchal times. Trade routes had been established and merchants from Babylonia and Assyria did a thriving business in Anatolia.

With the successful completion of the business transaction, the body of Sarah was placed in the cave which became the family burial place of Abraham. Although Abraham had been given promises which involved the possession of the land of Canaan by his descendants, the field which he purchased from Ephron was the only real estate which he personally owned during his lifetime.

15. A Wife for Isaac (24:1-67). Following the death of Sarah, Abraham was concerned about the future of Isaac, through whom the divine promises were to be realized.

a. The Servant's Commission (24:1-9). In view of the fact that Isaac was unmarried, and that a suitable wife could not be found among the neighboring Canaanites, a servant was sent to the region of Haran, where members of Abraham's family had settled, to find a suitable wife for Isaac. The servant is not named, but is generally assumed to be Eliezer (cf. Genesis 15:2).

According to Biblical idiom, children are said to issue from the "thigh" or "loins" of their father (cf. Genesis 46:26). Placing the hand on the thigh signified that, in the event that an oath were violated, the children who had issued, or might issue from the "thigh" would avenge the act of disloyalty. This has been called a "swearing by posterity," and is particularly applicable here, because the servant's mission is to insure a posterity for Abraham through Isaac.

To the servant's objection that he might not secure the consent of a suitable woman, Abraham replied that God would honor his covenant and provide the needed guidance and direction. In no case was a bride to be taken from the polytheistic tribes of Canaan.

b. The Servant at Nahor (24:10-61). The servant set out for Aram-naharaim (Mesopotamia) in an attitude of faith in Abraham's God. He carried with him presents for the prospective bride and her family. Arriving at "the city of Nahor," he prayed for guidance. Archaeological evidence locates a city named Nahor in the area of Paddan-Aram, or Aram-Naharaim, in which Haran is located. Nahor was the name of Abraham's brother. The name of the city is not spelled exactly like that of the man, but a relationship has been suggested. It is also possible that "the city of Nahor" simply means "the city in which Nahor lived" or Haran, itself.

In his prayer the servant proposed a test. If, on being asked for a drink of water, the young lady would not only provide water for the servant, but also for his camels, the servant would know that God had prospered his journey. The camel can go for days without water, but drinks much when it has the opportunity. The young lady who would offer to draw water for the camels would give evidence of an attitude of kindness which would reach even to the animals, and also evince a disposition to hard work.

Rebekah, the granddaughter of Nahor and the daughter of Bethuel, came to the well as the servant was praying, and her words and actions conformed perfectly to the pattern which would provide evidence of God's guidance. Being invited to lodge at the tent of Bethuel, the servant accepted the offered hospitality, made known his mission, and presented his gifts.

At the well, Abraham's servant gave Rebekah a nose ring and bracelets. When he entered the tent he gave her jewels and raiment expressive of the wealth and generosity of Abraham and Isaac. Presents were also given to Rebekah's mother and brother. These are known as the *mohar,* a kind of compensation to the family for the loss of the girl.

Rebekah's mother and brother suggested that she stay with them for a while before leaving. Ancient Jewish versions, including the Targum of Onkelos, suggest "a full year or ten months" (verse 35) as the time during which Rebekah's departure might be delayed.

The servant, however, was anxious to depart quickly. Upon being consulted, Rebekah agreed to leave immediately. With the blessing of Rebekah's family, the young lady, her nurse, and maids set out with Abraham's servant to begin a new life in Canaan.

c. Isaac and Rebekah (24:62-67). Isaac, who had been living in the Negeb, or South country, was meditating in the field when he heard the sound of the approaching caravan. Rebekah veiled herself when she learned that her prospective husband was in the field.

Learning of the providential hand of God in the matter, Isaac took Rebekah to his mother's tent, according to custom, and the marriage was consummated. The text adds that Isaac loved Rebekah and that he was "comforted for his mother," i.e., she filled the gap in his life caused by the death of his mother.

16. The Last Days of Abraham (25:1-11).

a. Abraham's Last Days (25:1-7). The statement that Abraham took Keturah as a wife does not necessarily imply that this event followed the death of Sarah. I Chronicles 1:32 calls Keturah a concubine, or secondary wife. She and her children are noted here because of the reference to the disposing of Abraham's property before his decease. It is, of course, possible that the sons of Keturah were born subsequent to the birth of Isaac, and that the miracle of Abraham's rejuvenation which enabled him to become the father of Isaac at the age of 100 was prolonged so that other sons might be born of Keturah.

Many of the descendants of Abraham through Keturah are recognizable as tribes of the north Arabian desert. The Midianites were nomads who are frequently mentioned in Scripture. Shuah is a progenitor of one of Job's friends, Bildad the Shuhite (Job 2:11).

Abraham divided his material wealth among his sons before his death. This was a wise precaution designed to prevent disputes and possible bloodshed later. With their gifts, the sons of the concubines went into the east country (*qedem*) where they continued to live a nomadic life. The Arab tribes are frequently called the "sons of the East" (*bᵉne qedem*).

Isaac became the heir, not only of the spiritual promises, but also of the bulk of Abraham's wealth. The portions alloted to the children of the concubines were termed "presents" whereas Isaac is named as "heir."

b. Abraham's Death and Burial (25:8-10). After a full life of 175 years Abraham died, and was buried by Isaac and Ishmael. It is encouraging to note the two half-brothers at the graveside of their father. They and their descendants frequently had differences, but the possibility of reconciliation and fellowship was never far removed.

The burial took place in the cave which Abraham had purchased from Ephron the Hittite. The families of Isaac and Jacob were subsequently buried in this family burial plot (cf. Genesis 49:30-32).

c. The Blessing of Isaac (25:11). It is significant that Isaac is not only named the heir of Abraham, but is also the recipient of a specific blessing from God. The promises made to Abraham are now transferred to Isaac.

17. The Descendants of Ishmael (25:12-18). The collateral line of Ishmael is disposed of before the focus of attention shifts to Isaac. Some of the descendants of Ishmael are well known from Assyrian and Arabian inscriptions. Nebaioth gives us the name Nabataean, the name of the tribe of Arabs which occupied the land of Edom in the two centuries before Christ. Petra was an important Nabataean city. Tema became an important center on the trade route from Yemen to Syria. Havilah is on the Persian Gulf, northeast of Arabia. It is noted for its gold (Genesis 2:11-12). The western extremity of the Ishmaelite settlements is Shur, the fortified settlement which the Egyptians maintained to keep out the eastern nomads.

B. (25:19—26:35) The Patriarch Isaac.

1. The Birth of Esau and Jacob (25:19-28). Scripture depicts Isaac as a transition figure, connecting Abraham and Jacob. Isaac's birth and early manhood are included in Abraham's biography. The remainder of Isaac's life story is linked with that of his twin sons, and especially with that of Jacob. These verses look backward to Abraham and forward to Esau and Jacob.

It is noteworthy that a second mother in succession in the line of the promised Seed is "barren." "Isaac entreated God" and "God was entreated" and Rebekah conceived. This underscores the fact that the Seed is provided by God.

Rebekah, puzzled by unusual symptoms, goes to God with her problem. God dispels her confusion by a reply of four poetic parallels: (1) Rebekah is to be the mother of twins who will be the progenitors of two nations, (2) the two children to be born shall develop into two separate nations, (3) the one nation should be stronger than the other, and (4) the elder would serve the younger.

At the time of delivery the twins were born in fulfillment of God's promise. There were further elements which pointed toward the fulfillment of the prophecy. There was striking physical differences in the twins, the first born being "ruddy" and "hairy" at birth (cf. 27:16), for which reason he was called Esau ("hairy"). The younger laid hold on the heel of the elder, from which he was named Jacob ("one who takes by the heel, the supplanter").

Also in early life the twins showed a disposition toward opposite pursuits. Esau became a lover of the out-of-doors, and was particularly loved by his father. Jacob, on the other hand, was the quiet tent-dweller, and appealed more to his mother, Rebekah. Thus the stage is set for the inevitable struggle.

2. The Sale of the Birthright (25:29-34). The concept of birthright in the line of Abraham involved both material and spiritual elements. In material things, the first-born could anticipate a double portion of the property which would be divided among his father's survivors. Neither Esau nor Jacob show much concern about spiritual matters in their early lives. Esau, however, is the "profane" man (i.e. worldly, living according to the dictates of the senses, who "despised his birthright."

Esau returned from a hunting expedition, faint from hunger. Jacob had prepared a kind of stew, or pottage, which hungry Esau desired. Jacob offered the pottage in exchange for Esau's birthright. Esau reasoned that the birthright would be useless if he were to starve to death, and accepted the bargain. His secular attitude and lack of faith in the God who had given His promises to Abraham and Isaac is the ground for his being termed "profane." Jacob's craftiness was not to go unpunished, however.

3. Isaac and Abimelech (26:1-16). The land of Palestine suffers from periodic famine. At such a time, Abraham had gone to Egypt in search of food. In the days of Joseph, Egypt would again be the granary of the surrounding lands. During the period of the Judges, Elimelech and Naomi went to Moab to find "bread" when there was famine in Bethlehem-Judah.

The conduct of Isaac in a time of famine parallels that of Abraham, although there are significant variations. Abimelech means "my father is king," or, more likely, "my father is Molech," the Canaanite deity who was worshipped by human sacrifice. In either event the term may be dynastic rather than personal. It may be compared with Pharaoh, the title given to the rulers of Egypt.

God appeared before Isaac in a theophany, assuring him that the covenant with Abraham would be fulfilled through Isaac. Obedience to God was enjoined.

Like his father before him, Isaac declared that his wife was his sister. Abimelech, however, observed him caressing her, whereupon he confronted Isaac with the charge of trying to conceal the truth.

Abimelech's conduct was exemplary. He guaranteed protection to Isaac and Rebekah. They were able to remain in the

Philistine country where their crops prospered. Flocks and herds multiplied until the Philistines envied Isaac and his family. The fact that this took place in a time of famine was evidence of God's blessing.

4. The Dispute over Wells (26:17-33). Jealousy between the herdsmen of Isaac and the herdsmen of Abimelech fomented such strife that Abimelech ordered Isaac to leave his district. Isaac did so, first settling in the *nahal* or *wady* of Gerar — evidently not far from Gerar itself. A *wady* is a river-bed which in the rainy season is a rushing stream, but in the dry summer is either a mere trickle of water or else entirely dry.

Isaac's servants dug wells which had been stopped up by the Philistines after Abraham's death. The "living water" (26:19) is water from a spring, as over against stagnant water which may come from a cistern.

The first of the wells was called Esek ("strife") because of the contention between the herdsmen of the rival leaders. The second was named Sitnah ("enmity") because of the continuing bitterness. A third, perhaps at a greater distance from the Philistine country, was named Rehoboth ("room") because the Philistines did not pursue Isaac's herdsmen to that well.

Moving on to Beer-sheba, Isaac experienced another theophany. God assured Isaac of His protecting care. Observing God's blessing on Isaac, Abimelech and his associates desired a covenant of friendship. This was accepted and sealed with a feast.

When the Philistines had peacefully departed from Isaac's camp, a reporter brought word of the discovery of another well, which was named "Shibah." Abraham had earlier given the name Beer-sheba to the site where the seven lambs were set aside in token of his rights to the area (cf. 21:29-31). It was thus "the well of the seven." To Isaac the name had the added significance of "the well of the oath." Both ideas are inherent in the name Beer-sheba.

5. Esau's Marriages (26:34-35). Esau's marriages are in harmony with his attitude in despising his birthright. Judith and Basemath are described as "Hittites," either because they are racially of Hittite origin or because they are natives of the land which frequently was called Hattu, or Hittite-land. The center of the Hittite culture was in Asia Minor, but Hittite influence reached down into Syria and Palestine at an early date. Intermarriage was contrary to the principles exemplified by Abraham

(cf. 24:3). Isaac and Rebekah grieved over Esau's compromising attitude.

C. (27:1—36:43) The Patriarch Jacob.

Jacob, or Israel, is the patriarch whose name is given to the nation which occupies the center of Bible history. The "children of Israel," or Israelites comprise twelve tribes, named for the twelve sons of Jacob, including the sons of Joseph whom Jacob adopted. The line of promise went from Abraham to Isaac, and from Isaac to Jacob, but no single son of Jacob is designated as the heir. The twelve sons became tribes, each of which functioned in the subsequent settlement of Canaan and the development of Israelite history.

1. The Blessing of Isaac (27:1-40). We are not told whether or not Isaac knew of the sale of the birthright. In any case he determined to bless his son Esau who was oldest in the family and the favorite of his father. The blessing was a form of a last will which was regarded as binding, even though orally pronounced. Nuzu tablets illustrate the binding nature of oral blessings.

While Esau was hunting venison to prepare for his father, Rebekah determined to secure the blessing for Jacob. Two "kids of the goats" were taken from the flock. Rebekah prepared them and helped to disguise Jacob so that he would have the smell and feel of his brother Esau. When Jacob appeared before Isaac, the latter was suspicious at the sound of the voice (27:22), but he felt the skins of the kids which had been placed on Jacob's hands and neck and decided that his suspicions were unfounded. The blessing meant for Esau was pronounced upon Jacob.

The blessing itself was generous in scope. The "dew of heaven" and the "fat places of the earth" were assigned to Jacob. The dew was essential to vegetation in Canaan, and its presence speaks of God's blessing. Similarly "fat" is emblematic of prosperity, as leanness speaks of poverty. The "peoples" or foreign nations would be subject to Jacob, and his own brethren (the related tribes) would own his lordship. The promise made by God to Abraham (12:3) was repeated by Isaac to Jacob.

When Esau presented himself to his father, expecting a blessing, he learned that Jacob had proved himself again to be "the supplanter." With tears he asked for some blessing (cf. Hebrews 12:17. Note that it was the blessing which he sought "with tears.").

The words of Isaac to Esau present a prophetic foreview of the history of the relations between Israel and Edom. Esau, or Edom, would live "by the sword." From the mountain strongholds, the Edomites would harass the more peaceful Israelites. Israel would rule Edom ("thou shalt serve thy brother,") but this rule would be of limited duration ("thou shalt shake his yoke from off thy neck").

2. The Reaction of Esau (27:41,42). Angered at the fact that Jacob had stolen the blessing, Esau determined to murder his brother. Since the death of Isaac was imminent, he determined only to delay his revenge until the period of mourning would be ended.

3. The Departure of Jacob (27:43—28:5). For two good reasons it was imperative that Jacob leave Canaan. Esau had determined to murder him, and Rebekah had learned of the plot. A brief sojourn in the area of Haran might be enough to allow things to calm down at home. In the meantime Jacob might find a suitable wife for himself in the area of Paddan-Aram. Rachel had come from that area. The local Hittite girls whom Esau had married were a source of grief to both Isaac and herself. With the blessing of Isaac, Jacob left for distant Paddan-Aram, expecting to be gone but a brief time (27:44). In fact Rebekah was never to see her favorite son again. More than twenty years would pass before he would return to Canaan.

4. Esau's Subsequent Marriage (28:6-9). Realizing that his prior marriages had been a source of grief to his parents, Esau married a daughter (or descendant) of Ishmael. Although the act shows a desire to please his parents, the Hittite wives continued to occupy their place in his harem, and an Ishmaelite would hardly be looked upon as a suitable wife for one who expected to live in the succession of the faithful.

5. Jacob's Dream of the Ladder (28:10-22). Enroute from Beer-sheba to Haran, Jacob spent the night near the ancient city of Luz. There, with a stone for a pillow, he dreamed of a ladder which reached heaven. Angels of God appeared, ascending and descending on the ladder. Although a fugitive in a strange land, Jacob learned that heaven was not far off. God was desirous of calling the wanderer to fellowship with Himself. The angels "ascending and descending" (cf. John 1:51), suggest that the way to fellowship with God is open to all who avail themselves of His grace.

In his dream, Jacob beheld a theophany. God appeared to Jacob with the promise that he and his seed would inherit the land of Canaan. God assured Jacob of his continuing care, and promised to bring him back to the land in which he was resting. In view of the trials which faced Jacob in his dealings with Laban, the promise must often have seemed vain. Yet God's Word could sustain Jacob in times of trial.

Upon awakening from his dream, Jacob named the place Bethel ("the house of God"). A pillar was erected as a monument to commemorate the spiritual experience of Jacob at Bethel. Jacob vowed to yield his life and a tenth of his possessions to God as his response to God's faithfulness to the divine promises which had been made at Bethel.

The pillar *(maṣṣēbah)* which Jacob erected was a memorial of the fact that God had appeared to him at Bethel. The concept of a memorial pillar appears as late as the time of Absalom (II Samuel 18:18) whose monument in the King's Vale could be seen at the time II Samuel was written ("unto this day"). Since pillars were an integral part of the debasing Canaanite religious rites, Israel was forbidden to erect them beside the altar of the Lord (Deuteronomy 16:22). Israel was enjoined to have no part in heathen worship: "Thou shalt not bow down to their gods, nor serve them, nor do after their doings; but thou shalt utterly overthrow them and break in pieces their pillars" (Exodus 23:24). Because of heathen associations all *masseboth* were denounced by the prophets (cf. Hosea 10:2).

6. Jacob Marries Leah and Rachel (29:1-30). Approaching a well in the region near Haran, the shepherds pointed out Rachel, the daughter of Laban, who was approaching with her sheep. Jacob removed the large stone which had been placed at the mouth of the well to protect the water from dust and sand. After introducing himself to Rachel as a son of Rebekah, Jacob was given a warm welcome by Laban, his mother's brother and Rachel's father.

Laban was the father of two girls. Leah, the elder, was "weak eyed" (rather than "tender eyed" — the description is not complimentary). Rachel, the younger daughter, was noted for her beauty. Jacob offered to serve Laban seven years for Rachel's hand. Laban agreed, and the years passed so swiftly for Jacob that they seemed "but a few days."

After seven years of labor, Jacob was ready to claim Rachel as his wife. Laban, however, fooled Jacob by veiling Leah and presenting her to Jacob in place of Rachel. Jacob had been guilty of trickery in his dealings with Isaac and Esau. He met his match in Laban, who protested that it was the custom of the land to marry off the eldest daughter first (29:26).

Although Jacob was incensed at Laban's conduct, he acceded to his request to complete the wedding week with Leah (29:27). Eight days after he married Leah, Jacob married Rachel on the understanding that he would serve Laban for another seven years. The week in verse 27 is the week of festivities in celebrating a marriage. Laban insisted that Jacob observe the proper proprieties during Leah's wedding week, after which arrangements were made for a second marriage. Jacob's love for Rachel has become proverbial. After her death it was revealed in the partiality he showed toward her two sons.

7. The Birth of Jacob's Sons (29:31–30:24). The sons of Jacob were born to his two wives, Leah and Rachel, and their two handmaids, Zilpah and Bilhah. Leah was the first to bear a son. This fact served as a kind of compensation for her lack of beauty. She was "hated" (i.e. "less loved") in contrast to the beloved Rachel. In God's providential government it is frequently true that those who are lacking in certain endowments are given others which more than compensate for the lack.

The names of Jacob's sons are listed, with the meaning of each name and an expression of faith on the part of the mother. The names should not be thought of as resulting from a careful study of etymology, but as the expression of the sentiments and hopes associated with the birth of each son.

The sons were born in the following order:

Mother	Name	Meaning and Explanation of the Name
Leah	Reuben	Behold, a son! Leah said, "The Lord hath looked on my affliction" (ra'ah be 'onyî).
	Simeon	Hearing (?). Leah said, "Because the Lord hath heard (shama') that I am hated, He hath given me this son also."
	Levi	Joined. Leah said, "This time will my husband be joined (yillaweh) unto me."
	Judah	May God be praised! Leah said, "This time will I praise ('ôdeh) the Lord."
Bilhah	Dan	A judge. Rachel, Bilhah's mistress, exclaimed, "God hath judged me (danani) and hath heard my voice and hath also given me a son."
	Naphtali	Wrestlings. Rachel said, "With mighty wrestlings (naphtulē 'elohîm) have I

71

Mother	Name	Meaning and Explanation of the Name
		wrestled *(niphtaltâ)* with my sister, and have prevailed."
Zilpah	Gad	Good fortune. Leah, Zilpah's mistress, said, "Fortune *(gad)* is come!"
	Asher	Happiness. Leah said, "Happy *('asher)* am I."
Leah	Issachar	Hire. Leah said, "God hath given me my hire *(sekarî)* because I gave my handmaid to my husband."
	Zebulon	Honor (?). Leah said, "God hath endowed me with a good dowry; now will my husband honor me (i.e., not dismiss me) *(zebalanî)*, because I have borne him six sons."
Rachel	Joseph	May He (the Lord) add! Rachel said, "God hath taken away *('asaph)* my reproach . . . may the Lord add *(yoseph)* to me another son." Two Hebrew roots are used here in a word-play on the name of Joseph.
	Benjamin (Gen. 35)	Son of the right hand. Rachel, who died in giving birth to Benjamin, called him Ben-oni ("son of my sorrow"). Jacob, however, called him Benjamin in token of his favored position.

It is clear (cf. 37:35) that Jacob had numerous daughters. Only one is mentioned, Dinah, whose rape by the Shechemites is mentioned in chapter 34 as the occasion which produced serious problems for the family of Jacob.

The mandrakes (30:14-16) *(duda'im)* are, by popular etymology, associated with the Hebrew *dôd,* love, or beloved. They are sometimes called "love apples." The fleshy forked root of the mandrake resembles the lower part of the human body. This fact seems to account for the aphrodisiac qualities attributed to the mandrake from ancient times. The fruit is the size of a large plum, yellow in color, and full of soft pulp. It is still valued in the East as a love charm.

Rachel, concerned about her sterility, learned that Leah's son, Reuben, had found some mandrakes in the field during the wheat harvest. When Rachel, who held the superstitious view that mandrakes would serve as a remedy for her barrenness, asked Leah for some, the evils of polygamous society became obvious.

Leah charges Rachel with alienation of affection ("Is it a small thing that thou hast taken away my husband?"). Leah obviously feels that the possession of mandrakes will give Rachel a still greater advantage. If childless Rachel is Jacob's favorite, what will be his attitude toward his wives if both of them have children? Nevertheless a bargain is struck, and Leah yielded some of her son's mandrakes to Rachel.

Rachel's bargaining for the mandrakes did not produce the desired result, however. Leah gave birth to Issachar, Zebulon, and Dinah, but Rachel remained barren. Divine providence rather than human superstition produces fertility. In due time, "God remembered Rachel and God hearkened unto her and opened her womb." Israel was influenced by the superstitious ideas of her neighbors, but the Bible makes it clear that God was directly operative in her history. The record of superstitious practices in Scripture must not be confused with the approval of such practices.

8. Laban's Wages (30:25-43). After a period of fourteen years, during which Jacob served Laban for Leah and Rachel, he determined to return to Canaan. Had he left at this time, he would have returned with no possessions except for his wives and family.

a. Jacob's Proposal (30:25-33). At Jacob's request to be permitted to return home, Laban offered to negotiate terms whereby Jacob might continue to work for him for "wages." Jacob had been faithful in his work, and the blessing of God had rested upon him. Laban had consulted some type of omens (nihashti) which led him to believe that he should retain Jacob in his employ. Laban's question, "What shall I give thee?" is an invitation to Jacob to set his own price for his continued employ as Laban's shepherd.

Jacob actually stipulated a very small wage. Palestinian sheep are almost all white; goats are normally black. Jacob specified that he would accept as his wages the speckled, spotted, and black among the sheep, and the speckled and spotted among the goats. The proposal involved present animals in those categories, and those which should afterwards be born. Although asking little for himself, Jacob's proposal had the merit of providing a positive test of integrity. The flocks of Laban could be distinguished from those of Jacob at a glance.

b. Laban's Deceit (30:34-36). Laban, with no grounds for suspecting Jacob of dishonesty, proceeded to divide the flocks with a view to increasing his own holdings at the expense of

Jacob. The reference to "his sons" (30:35) appears to refer to the sons of Laban rather than the sons of Jacob. Although no sons of Laban are mentioned up to this point, it is clear from 31:1 that there were such. The reference in 30:34-36 is understandable if Laban's own sons are in view.

Jacob had suggested that *he* would remove the abnormally colored sheep and goats from the flock (30:32) but Laban hastily ("that day") removed them and committed them into the care of his own sons in order to outwit Jacob. When Jacob would come to the flock in order to take the portion which had been agreed upon for his own possession, he would find that nothing, or very little, would fit into the category which he had generously suggested.

Laban's initial fear of losing the valuable services of Jacob had lost its force by this time. Since Jacob has accepted terms for remaining in Paddan-Aram, Laban is again ready to exploit the situation for his own wealth.

c. Jacob's Counter-Deceit (30:37-43). The dealings of Jacob with Laban involved a continual battle of wits. Jacob's initial suggestion of a means of dividing the flock involved an attitude of faith in God. Faced with a fresh example of Laban's craftiness, however, Jacob devised three methods to insure the size and quality of the flocks he desired:

(1) He placed streaked rods where they would be seen by the ewes in order that the coloring of the young might be subject to pre-natal influence (30:37).

(2) Jacob separated the newly born spotted lambs and kids from the rest of the flock, but so arranged them that there would be a further tendency to bear spotted young (30:40).

(3) He devised means to secure for himself the young of the strongest animals (30:41).

Jacob saw fit to manipulate the portion of Laban's flock which had not been entrusted to his sons. Selective breeding and prenatal influence are methods which Jacob adopted. The multiplication of Jacob's flocks, however, is attributed by the sacred historian to the intervention of God (cf. 31:12). The means which Jacob adopted were overruled by God to accomplish His purposes.

As Oswald T. Allis notes, this incident should not be appealed to as proof that the Bible supports the theory of pre-natal influence. He observes, "The means to which Jacob resorted to secure the fulfillment of the dream may have been quite as unnecessary to the fulfillment of God's purpose as was Abraham's marriage to Hagar" *(God Spake by Moses,* p. 42).

In their article, "Biology and Creation" in *Modern Science and the Christian Faith,* W. J. Tinkle and W. E. Lammerts comment, "To the casual observer they [i.e., the flock Jacob tended] were of solid colors, for all the spotted goats had been removed; but their hereditary factors or genes for color were mixed, the condition which geneticists call heterozygous. At this point modern genetics helps us, for breeding tests have shown that spotting is recessive to solid color in goats, making it possible for a goat to have spots that can be transmitted, although they do not appear to the eye."

The Christian sees God as normally using the forces of nature and of history to accomplish His purposes. He is in no sense limited to those forces, however.

9. The Flight of Jacob (31:1-21). Jacob's final determination to leave Paddan-Aram is attributable to two causes. Jacob's increasing prosperity had resulted in jealousy on the part of Laban's sons and increasing hostility from Laban himself. This was in marked contrast to Laban's earlier desire to profit from Jacob's faithful service as a shepherd. If any doubt lingered in Jacob's mind, his future course was made clear in a dream during which God, who identified Himself as the God of Bethel, commanded him to return to the land of his birth. A combination of human reasoning and divine revelation impelled Jacob to act quickly.

Revealing his plan to his wives, Jacob took advantage of Laban's absence to make a secret departure. His family and possessions, including the large flocks which he had acquired while working for Laban, started on the long journey across the Euphrates to the land of Canaan.

Before leaving, Rachel stole the *teraphim* (verse 19) or "household gods" (cf. verse 30) of her father Laban. The Nuzu tablets indicate that the *teraphim* prove that their possessor is the proper heir of the family. It would appear that Laban had no male heir at the time Jacob first came to Paddan-Aram. When Jacob married Leah and Rachel he would be adopted by his father-in-law, assuming the duties of a son and being designated as Laban's heir. At Nuzu, the birth of a natural son reduced the status of an adopted son, although the latter had certain rights which had to be respected. The subsequent birth of natural sons to Laban meant that Jacob's position in the household was radically changed. Jacob would no longer be

Laban's chief heir, for natural sons take precedence over adopted sons. Rachel, however, determined to maintain the position of primacy for herself and her husband. To keep the birthright from falling to a younger brother, she stole the *teraphim*. Jacob was totally ignorant of Rachel's act. He had his own birthright in the family of Isaac, and was evidently willing to relinquish his position as Laban's adopted son.

10. **Laban's Pursuit (31:22-42).** When Laban learned of Jacob's flight he pursued him until he reached Jacob's caravan in the mountains of Gilead. There Laban was warned by God to speak "neither good nor bad" to Jacob. Opposites in Scripture frequently express totality. Laban was ordered to say nothing to Jacob. He was not to challenge him or interfere with his plans.

The meeting between Laban and Jacob was in accord with the spirit, at least, of this command. Laban professed to have been grieved because he did not have the opportunity to provide a suitable farewell for his family. He mentions his "sons." There were no actual sons of Laban with Jacob, but in normal Semitic usage the term "son" indicates a male descendant, immediate or remote. In this instance the "sons" were Laban's grandsons. Similarly the term "daughters" would include Leah and Rachel, Dinah, and any other granddaughters. In a less friendly tone, evidently forgetting the divine command, Laban asked, "Wherefore hast thou stolen my gods?" (i.e. the *teraphim*).

Jacob assured his father-in-law that he had left secretly for fear that Laban would not permit Leah and Rachel to leave. As patriarch of his tribe, Laban had certain rights over his daughters even after their marriage. To avoid a possible showdown, Jacob had secretly departed.

Concerning the *teraphim,* Jacob insisted that he knew nothing. He gave Laban permission to search the camp, suggesting the death penalty for the thief. The Code of Hammurabi, the Old Babylonian lawgiver, specifies that anyone who stole the property of a god or temple should die. It was because Jacob was certain that the *teraphim* were not in his camp that he spoke so boldly.

Laban searched the camp, but he did not find the *teraphim*. When he approached Rachel, who was seated on her camel, she asked to be excused from arising because of the fact that she was pregnant. "The manner of women is upon me," she said (31:35). Actually she had hidden the *teraphim* in a little box

76

which formed part of the saddle of the camel on which she was riding. Such saddles are pictured on reliefs from the ancient Near East (see J. B. Pritchard, *The Ancient Near East in Pictures*, fig. 188).

Jacob was angered at Laban for making a charge which seemed but an excuse for searching the caravan. He eloquently described his faithful work as Laban's shepherd (31:38-40). According to the Code of Hammurabi, a shepherd gave a receipt for the animals entrusted to him. A certain number might be used for food. The shepherd was not responsible for those killed by lions or by lightning. He was expected to return the flock with reasonable increase, and any loss due to his own carelessness had to be repaid tenfold.

Jacob assured Laban that he had been prospered because "the God of my father, the God of Abraham, and the Fear of Isaac" had been on his side. The "Fear of Isaac" is the One whom Isaac feared, his God. Jacob accused Laban of having changed his wages "ten times" during the twenty years of their association. The "ten" in this context is equivalent to "time after time," or "many times."

11. The Covenant between Jacob and Laban (31:43-54). Laban, professing to be concerned about the welfare of his daughters and grandchildren, suggested a solemn covenant which would prevent Jacob from returning to Paddan-Aram to seek revenge for the injustices to which he had been exposed while in Laban's household.

Jacob agreed to enter such a covenant. He set up a "pillar" and suggested that his kinsmen gather stones which appear to have been heaped around the "pillar." A covenant sacrifice was then eaten (cf. 26:30).

The "heap" of stones was given a dual name, reflecting the Aramaic tongue of Laban and the Hebrew language of Jacob. We are not told what language Abraham spoke while in Ur, but the branch of the family that settled in the area of Haran evidently spoke Aramaic. Abraham and his successors, after their entry into Canaan appear to have adopted a Canaanite dialect which is known to us as Hebrew.

The "Heap of Witness" was, to Laban, *Jegar-sahadutha,* and to Jacob, *Gal 'ed.* A further name, *Mizpah* ("watch-post") was given to the place. Mizpah becomes a kind of sentry to keep watch on Jacob and Laban when they cannot keep watch on one another.

Laban insisted that the "pillar" and "heap" be witness that neither of the parties to the covenant would pass the spot intent on harm to the other. Jacob was happy to agree. The episode was concluded with a sacrificial feast of thanksgiving.

12. Jacob's Encounter with Esau (32:1—33:15). On his journey homeward from Paddan-Aram, Jacob had to anticipate trouble from two directions. Laban had appeared to challenge Jacob's hasty exodus, but serious trouble had been averted. A covenant was made with a view to assuring peaceful relations between the families of Jacob and Laban.

Another source of possible trouble was that which stemmed from Jacob's defrauding of Esau in the years before Jacob's sojourn in Paddan-Aram. Esau had earlier threatened the life of Jacob. Jacob was concerned about his present attitude. Would he still seek vengeance? As Jacob came nearer to the land of his birth, his concern about Esau assumed gigantic proportions. Before he could meet his estranged brother, Jacob needed a spiritual experience of God's presence and power.

a. Jacob Encouraged by Angels (32:1-3). Entering the Land of Promise, the angels of God met Jacob. These heavenly ministrants were preparing Jacob for the ordeal which he dreaded. Jacob was returning to Canaan in the will of God, and God's angels provided a guarantee of providential blessing.

Jacob called the place where the angels appeared to him Mahanaim ("two camps"). He appears to think of the two hosts with which God has blessed him — his own camp, and the host of angels. He was aware that his own camp was in imminent danger, but looked upon the angelical host as heavenly provision for all that might lie ahead.

b. Jacob Prepares to Meet Esau (32:4-24). The assurance of God's blessing did not deter Jacob from using means, but rather provided the needed spur to encourage him to act quickly. Jacob determined to send messengers to Edom, where Esau lived. The messengers were commanded to speak in a humble and conciliatory way. Jacob had sojourned with Laban, had been detained *('ēḥar)*, but was now returning with evidences of God's blessing. Bad news reached Jacob, however. Esau and four hundred of his men were marching toward Jacob's camp.

Jacob made both spiritual and material preparation for the dreaded encounter. The spiritual preparation is recorded in verses 10-13. In prayer, Jacob gave evidence of humility and gratitude toward God for the blessings of the past and the promises for the future. The prayer breathes an attitude of faith. Jacob admits his fear of Esau, but trusts God as his deliverer. The years of suffering in Paddan-Aram were not in vain as far as Jacob's spiritual life is concerned.

Physical preparation involved two factors. The camp was divided into two sections (32:8) so that half might be preserved if Esau should ruthlessly fall upon one of the camps. To avert such a disaster, Jacob provided a series of gifts which were designed to appease Esau and secure his good will. In all, 580 beasts were sent as a present to Esau. Jacob tarried in the camp.

c. Jacob Wrestles with a "Man" (32:25-32). Continuing his journey, Jacob escorted his wives, handmaids, and children across the ford of the Jabbok (the *Wady-ez-Zerka*), after which he returned to the north bank of the stream. He may have been making a routine check to be sure that all had been conveyed to the south shore when, alone, in a solitary spot, he met a strange "man."

The night battle between Jacob and the "man" who wrestled with him by the Jabbok was a great crisis in the life of the progenitor of the Israelites. This "man" who suddenly appeared in the dark of night was no mere mortal. He had the power to bless. He conveyed a new name. Jacob was convinced that he had striven "with God" that night (32:32). The prophet Hosea (12:4) provides a commentary on the episode.

In this night battle, Jacob learned his own helplessness. To overcome Jacob, his mysterious assailant "touched the hollow" of his thigh. The ball-and-socket joint was dislocated by a mere touch. In the morning, Jacob went limping away (32:32). God had prevailed over Jacob. The supplanter (as the name Jacob implies) had become the "Champion of God" *(Yisra'el)*. He had striven *(sarah)* with God and men, and had emerged victorious.

If God had prevailed over Jacob, it was no less true that Jacob had prevailed "with God." Jacob knew that he needed a blessing. In anxiety of soul he sought it, and God granted it unto him.

It would be too much to say that Israel never descended to the level of the old Jacob again. The names Israel and Jacob both appear in the subsequent narrative — and, indeed, in the poetical and prophetic literature of the Old Testament. Yet it is true that Jacob could never forget this experience at the Jabbok. It marked a turning point in his life.

Jacob gave the name Peniel (or Penuel) to the place of his encounter. Peniel means "the face of God." During his midnight ordeal, Jacob had seen God. He left with a limp and a blessing.

A commemoration of Jacob's encounter at the Jabbok is preserved in Jewish dietary restrictions. The sciatic nerve, or thigh-vein, must be removed from the slaughtered animal before that portion of the animal may be prepared for consumption by orthodox Jews.

d. Jacob and Esau Meet (33:1-15). Jacob made elaborate preparation for his encounter with Esau. Arranging in order the handmaids and their children and the wives with their children, Jacob desired his brother to meet the caravan in a kind of climactic order. The best was reserved for the last place. This also served a practical function. If Esau approached with hostile intent, those at the rear would be more likely preserved than those at the front.

In oriental style, illustrated frequently in the Amarna tablets, Jacob greeted Esau by bowing before him seven times. The meeting of the brothers who had been estranged twenty years before proved to be a glad reunion. Jacob insisted that Esau accept the gift which had been provided. Esau insisted that he had an abundance of possessions and could not accept Jacob's present. On Jacob's continual insistence, Esau complied. Failure to have accepted the gift would have been interpreted as an insult and the strained relations between the brothers would have continued.

The actual encounter between Jacob and Esau was very brief. Esau seems to have advanced toward Jacob with hostile intent. When Esau saw his brother and the evidences of God's blessing on Jacob, his fraternal feeling overcame his desire for revenge. Esau suggested that the two companies travel southward together. The young children and the flocks of Jacob's caravan would make very slow travelling, however. Jacob suggested that Esau travel on ahead, suggesting that they would later meet at Mt. Seir. This may have subsequently occurred, although we have no Scriptural record of it.

Jacob's words, "I have seen thy face as one seeth the face of God" (verse 10), are not words of flattery. Jacob saw a kindness in Esau's face which was evidence that God had wrought forgiveness in Esau's heart. Esau's face then bore "a reflection of the Divine kindness" (Delitzsch).

13. Jacob in Canaan (33:16—35:20).

a. Jacob Settles in Canaan (33:16-20). Staying for a short time at a place called Succoth, Jacob settled near Shechem on his arrival in the land of Canaan. To secure his right to the property, a parcel of ground was purchased for one hundred pieces of money. This is the second record of land purchase by the patriarchs (cf. John 4:5).

Jacob built an altar at his new piece of property. The name he gave to it is expressive of his own new name: *'El 'Elohē Israel —.'El* (God), the God of Israel. Among the Canaanites, Jacob raised up a testimony to the God who had brought him back to the land of his birth.

b. Dinah and the Men of Shechem (34:1-31). The humbling and avenging of Dinah is one of those sordid chapters of history which show mankind at its worst. Sin begets sin, and the way of the transgressor inevitably leads to ruin.

A man named Shechem, the son of Hamor, by brute strength seized and had illicit relations with Dinah, a daughter of Leah and Jacob (30:21). Desiring a permanent relationship, Hamor, Shechem's father, investigated the possibilities of intermarriage. The sons of Jacob mentioned the requirement of circumcision, and deceitfully suggested that intermarriage might be arranged between members of the two groups if the sons of Hamor would submit to the rite.

When the men of the city were in a weakened condition as a result of their circumcision, Simeon and Levi, the full brothers of Dinah, entered the city and killed all of the men, including Hamor and Shechem. They took all of the possessions of the men of the city as spoil.

Jacob properly rebuked Simeon and Levi for this outrage. Two wrongs never make a right. The episode is referred to in Jacob's blessing (49:5). In avenging their sister's honor, Simeon and Levi compromised the testimony of Jacob and his sons in the land of Canaan, and exposed them to needless hostility from the inhabitants of the land.

c. Back to Bethel (35:1-15). Jacob's earlier experience at Bethel was that of a fugitive seeking to escape the wrath of an angry brother. Now he is a fugitive again. The rash action of Simeon and Levi has put him on the defensive among his Canaanite neighbors. God instructed him to return to Bethel.

Many of the servants of Jacob seem to have been idolaters. Jacob insisted that the idols (including, no doubt, the *teraphim* which Rachel had taken from Laban) and idolatrous ornaments be gathered together and buried under a Terabinth tree. God protected him from the wrath of the Canaanites as he journeyed from Shechem to Bethel.

At Bethel, Jacob built an altar which he named El-bethel ("The God of Bethel" or "The God of the House of God"). Here God appeared to Jacob and repeated the promises which had been made to Abraham and Isaac. At Bethel, Jacob erected a memorial pillar on which he poured a drink-offering and oil. The monument erected at Jacob's earlier visit (28:18) would hardly be standing after a lapse of thirty years.

The earlier experience at Bethel had been a purely personal one. Here his family is represented. They learn the meaning of the name of Bethel. A note of sorrow is injected in the mention of Deborah, Rebekah's nurse, who died while the family of Jacob sojourned there.

The experience at Bethel was needed by Jacob after his difficulties with the Canaanites which resulted from the murder of Shechem and Hamor. God, who had appeared to Jacob in early life at Bethel, confirmed the promises then made and assured Jacob of continuing blessing.

d. The Death of Rachel and the Birth of Benjamin (35:16-20). To the end, Rachel remained the beloved wife of Jacob. South of Bethel at Ephrath she gave birth to a son, but died in childbirth. In her hour of sorrow, Rachel named the infant Ben-oni ("son of my sorrow"), but Jacob named him Benjamin ("son of my right hand"). The right hand is considered to be the position of honor.

The tomb of Rachel at Bethlehem symbolizes the tender side of the life of Jacob. With Rachel's death, her two sons, Joseph and Benjamin, receive all the love and affection of Jacob.

A memorial monument was lovingly erected by Jacob at the grave of Rachel which was still intact when the book of Genesis was written. On the right side of the road from Jerusalem to Bethlehem the traditional tomb of Rachel may still be seen. The present structure was built by the Crusaders when they occupied Bethlehem in the twelfth century. The site was alluded to by Jerome in the fourth century.

The prophet Jeremiah pictures Rachel as interested in the future of her children: "A voice is heard in Ramah, lamentation and bitter weeping, Rachel weeping for her children; She refuseth to be comforted for her children, because they are not" (Jeremiah 31:15). The children of Rachel were soon to die or go into exile at the hand of the Babylonians. Jeremiah adds, "Refrain thy voice from weeping, and thine eyes from tears; for thy work shall be rewarded, saith the Lord, and they shall come back from the land of the enemy" (31:16). God will not utterly cast off his people, Jeremiah says. There will be a restoration following the exile. Matthew (2:18-19) quotes Jeremiah's prophecy of weeping Rachel in connection with Herod's massacre of the infants of Bethlehem. Rachel is concerned with the lot of her children when they are suffering under the hand of Herod, as she was concerned when they were suffering under Nebuchadnezzar, or the Assyrians. Jeremiah's words assume new proportions when infants are slaughtered by one who is jealous of One who was born "king of the Jews."

In I Samuel 10:2, Rachel's sepulchre is located "in the border of Benjamin at Zelzah." The border between Benjamin and Judah ran diagonally through Jerusalem. The exact location of Zelzah is not known. Ramah is five miles north of Jerusalem. Ramah means "heights" however, and Ramah in Benjamin may not be the intended place. Rachel died on the way to Bethlehem and, presumably, was buried not far from Bethlehem.

14. Resumé: Jacob's Twelve Sons (35:21-26). It was the practice among heirs to the throne to take possession of their father's wives as an assertion of their right to succession. Greed as well as lust may have prompted Reuben to have sinful relations with Bilhah, his father's concubine. Jacob's disapproval is evident from 49:4 where he makes it clear that Reuben, by his sinful act, has forfeited his rights as firstborn.

15. Death and Burial of Isaac (35:27-29). Since the focus of attention in the subsequent history will be on Jacob, the death and burial of Isaac are recorded here. As Isaac and Ishmael had been present for the funeral rites of Abraham, so Esau and Jacob are together at the burial of Isaac (cf. 25:8). Isaac forms a transition between Abraham and Jacob. His life was neither as rough nor as eventful as those of his father and son.

16. The Family of Esau (36:1-19). Although not the heir to the promises, a blessing had been pronounced on Esau (27:39-40). Here his genealogy is given. In subsequent years hostility existed between Edomites and Israelites. Israel is reminded, however, that they are blood relatives with the descendants of Esau.

The names of Judith and Basemath occur as wives of Esau in 26:34. Apparently Judith is to be identified with Oholibamah, and Basemath with Ada. The use of names was quite fluid in the ancient orient. Women frequently received a new name at marriage.

17. The Original Inhabitants of Edom (36:20-30). Before the family of Esau settled at Mt. Seir it was occupied by Horites, a people now identified with the Hurrians, whose language and culture have been the object of intensive study in recent years. Hurrian scribes wrote the Nuzu tablets which have thrown much light on social conditions in Mesopotamia in the patriarchal age. Most of their writing is in Accadian cuneiform, but the Hurrian language is known, and a grammar has been written by Ephraim Speiser of the University of Pennsylvania. The Hurrians were non-Semitic (cf. Deuteronomy 2:12).

18. The Kings of Edom (36:31-43). The listing of "kings" of Edom evokes the comment that the Edomites had rulers known as kings before such rulers were known in Israel. In 35:11 God had promised Jacob, "kings shall come out of thy loins." Before such a promise was fulfilled among the descendants of Jacob, Esau's line developed the institution of royalty. Interpreted in this way, the words may be attributed to Moses.

It is, of course, possible that the words "before there reigned any king over the children of Israel" are a later editorial interpolation. Belief in the Mosaic authorship of the pentateuch does not deny the possibility of editorial revision by Ezra, or some other inspired writer at a later period.

In accord with the style of Genesis, the collatoral line of Esau is briefly discussed before attention is focused on God's dealings with the main line, in this case the family of Jacob.

D. (37:1—50:26) The Patriarch Joseph.

1. Joseph and His Brothers (37:1-36). The history of Joseph and his relations with his father and brothers serve as an example of that interaction of human freedom and divine sovereignty which characterizes the whole of Biblical history. Each individual acts in an atmosphere of freedom and responsibility, yet the totality of those acts brings about the sovereign purpose of the God Who is both above history and in history.

a. Joseph at Home (37:1-4). Jacob's home exhibits some of the evils of polygamous society. Two wives and two concubines had given birth to twelve sons and an unmentioned number of daughters. Joseph, the firstborn son of Rachel, Jacob's favorite wife, held a position of special honor. Rachel's death in giving birth to Benjamin also served to make her particularly dear to Jacob. Favored by Jacob, Joseph became increasingly unpopular with his brothers. Two reasons for this are noted.

As a lad of seventeen, Joseph accompanied his half-brothers, the sons of the handmaids Bilhah and Zilpah, when they were tending the sheep. Joseph brought to his father an "evil report" of their behavior, a fact which would naturally build resentment in their minds against him. Ehrlich suggests that Jacob had appointed Joseph to supervise his brothers, translating: "Joseph, being seventeen years old, used to supervise — although only a lad — his brethren, viz., the sons of Bilhah and the sons of Zilpah (when they were) with the sheep."

A special coat, translated "coat of many colors" (following the Septuagint and Targum Jonathan) was given to Joseph by his father. Hebraists variously describe Joseph's *kethoneth passim* as a tunic reaching to the ankles or a tunic composed of variegated pieces. The interpretation of the Septuagint seems to be borne out by the Bene Hassan tomb paintings which show a caravan of Semites arriving in Egypt (c. 1900 B.C.) with tribal leaders wearing coats of many colors (see J. B. Pritchard, *The Ancient Near East in Pictures,* fig. 3). Joseph's coat marked him as the one who would succeed his father as chief of the tribes. Second Samuel 13:18 indicates that members of the royal family wore such garments as late as David's time.

b. Joseph's Dreams (37:5-11). The dreams of Joseph indicated that he would one day hold a position of authority over his brothers. The imagery of the first dream is that of agricultural Palestine. Sheaves had been tied. That belonging to Joseph arose, and the sheaves of Joseph's brothers gathered around and bowed before it. When Joseph told his brothers of his dream they were incensed at the thought that he should rule over them.

The second dream involved the heavenly bodies. The sun, moon, and eleven stars bowed before Joseph. This was more inclusive than the first. Joseph has pre-eminence over his father and (now dead) mother as well as his brothers.

Jacob's reaction was mixed. He rebuked Joseph for this declaration of his pre-eminence over all the family. Perhaps Joseph was unwise in the way in which he related his dreams. His youthful guilelessness did not envision the jealousy of his brothers.

It was clear, however, that Jacob was impressed. He "kept the saying in mind." Uncertain about the meaning of the dream, he nevertheless must have felt some sense of satisfaction. Joseph was his favorite son. Did God intend to bestow some signal honor on him? Joseph's dreams need not be thought of

85

as different in kind from other dreams, but they were "divinely controlled so as to express what afterward actually transpired" (Leupold).

c. Joseph's Brothers (37:12-28).

(1) Joseph Sent to Them (37:12-17). In a nomadic or semi-nomadic society, mobility is a prime factor. In quest for good pasture land it may be necessary to move far from a home base. Jacob, desirous of learning of the welfare of his sons and the flocks which they tended, sent Joseph from the Hebron area, where Jacob made his home (35:27) to Shechem, where the brothers had gone in search for good pasture land. The region of Shechem was a fertile plain. Joseph's brothers, however, found it advisable to move farther north to Dothan, currently being excavated by the Wheaton Archaeological Expedition under the direction of Joseph P. Free.

(2) They Conspire against Him (37:18-20). When his brothers saw Joseph approaching the rich pasture lands of Dothan they determined to rid themselves of "this dreamer." They planned to slay him, leaving his body in a nearby pit. They would account for his death by blaming it on the wild beasts which roamed central Palestine in patriarchal days.

(3) Reuben's Plan (37:21-24). Reuben determined to rescue Joseph. He knew the determination of his brothers to kill Joseph, however. To prevent immediate action by the hostile brothers, Reuben made a proposal which would, at least temporarily, save Joseph's life.

"Do not shed blood," Reuben urged. The pits, or cisterns in which water was stored, had narrow openings so that anyone imprisoned in them could not get out without assistance. "Put Joseph in this cistern," Reuben suggested. He hoped to persuade the hostile brothers that it would be better to allow Joseph to starve to death in the cistern than to murder him in cold blood. Reuben planned, however, at an opportune moment to rescue him. Although Reuben's plan did not succeed in securing Joseph's release, it did spare his life. Joseph was stripped of his coat and cast into the dry cistern.

(4) Joseph Sold to the Ishmaelites (37:25-28). Dothan lay on the trade route which ran from Gilead, east of the Jordan, across the Valley of Jezreel, down the Philistine coast, to Egypt. In the clear Palestinian air a caravan could be seen many miles away. In the absence of Reuben, Judah suggested that the brothers might sell Joseph to a passing caravan. Thus, in-

stead of being permitted to die in an abandoned cistern, Joseph could be sold into slavery.

The merchant caravan is variously described as Ishmaelite, Midianite, and Medanite (a variant of Midianite). Ishmaelites and Midianites are descendants of Abraham. Their appearance and characteristics were so similar that a given caravan might be described by both names. Leupold suggests that the Ishmaelites may have been the dominant faction, the Midianites the most numerous.

An alternate view suggests that the brothers were thwarted in their plans to sell Joseph for a profit to the Ishmaelite caravan by some passing Midianite merchants. This view, suggested by Koenig and held by Rabbi Hertz, suggests that the Midianites, hearing human cries from the pit, lifted Joseph out of the pit and sold him to the Ishmaelites. Those who maintain this view note that Joseph later described himself as having been "stolen away out of the land of the Hebrews" (40:15).

d. The Deception of Jacob (37:29-35). Reuben, who seems to have been away during the time when the Ishmaelites and Midianites appeared, went to the pit in order to release Joseph, but found it empty. In dismay he turned to his brothers, exclaiming, "The child is not; and as for me, whither shall I go?" Reuben, as the firstborn, would be held responsible for Joseph's welfare. Reuben knew that his father would be angry with him.

The brothers agreed on means whereby Jacob would be deceived. They dipped Joseph's coat in the blood of a goat. Bringing it to Jacob, they implied that Joseph had never reached them at Dothan. "This have we found," they explained, "Know now whether it is thy son's coat or not."

Jacob identified the coat. In earlier life he had been a deceiver. Isaac, Esau, and, in measure at least, Laban had been deceived by the craftiness of Jacob. Now, with horrible justice, the deceiver was deceived. Refusing to be comforted, Jacob insisted that he would go to the grave mourning the death of his favorite son.

e. Joseph Sold into Egypt (37:36). The hand of God is evident in the details of Joseph's experience in Egypt. He became a slave in the household of an important officer of the reigning pharaoh. This was the first step in the tortuous road to the office of Prime Minister.

The title "captain of the guard" *(sar hattabahîm)* may literally be translated "chief of the executioners." The term is used of the king's body-guard. The name "Potiphar" means "The gift of Ra" (the Egyptian sun-god).

2. Judah and Tamar (38:1-30). Although the episodes of chapter 38 interrupt the account of Joseph in Egypt, they are in no sense an intrusion. From the narrative point of view they create suspense by delaying the answer to the question, "What happened to Joseph in Egypt?" The conduct of Judah when in a place of temptation forms a fitting contrast to that of Joseph when beset by a somewhat similar enticement.

a. Judah Marries Shua (38:1-5). Intermarriage with the Canaanites was the cause of grief during much of the history of Israel. Esau had been guilty of contracting marriage with the heathen who lived nearby (26:34), a fact which brought sorrow to Isaac and Rebekah.

Shua, described as "a daughter of a certain Canaanite," bore three sons to Judah: Er, Onan, and Shelah.

b. Tamar's Two Marriages (38:6-10). In accord with the marriage customs of the day, Judah secured a wife for Er, his oldest son. Tamar, the wife, was soon left a widow. As a result of some unmentioned act of sin, Er died without leaving an heir. In such cases the custom of levirate marriage was observed. A surviving brother-in-law was expected to marry the childless widow, and the oldest son of this marriage would inherit the name and property of the deceased brother. The principle is declared in Deuteronomy 25:5 and illustrated in Ruth 4:5-6.

Onan was willing to marry his brother's widow, but he refused to make possible the birth of a child. The judgment of God fell upon him and he, too, died.

c. Judah Defrauds Tamar of her Marriage Rights (38:11). Tamar, through marriage, had become a member of Judah's household. In the absence of a husband, she would be required to render obedience to him. He, on the other hand, was obligated to observe the custom of levirate marriage and provide a husband for Tamar. This he refused to do, feeling that she was in some way responsible for the death of two of his sons. Hypocritically he ordered Tamar to remain a widow at the home of her father until Shelah should reach manhood. Actually he had no intention of permitting the marriage.

d. Tamar Deceives Judah (38:12-23). Tamar learned that Judah, who had in the meantime become a widower, was going to Timnah, a few miles south of Hebron, to see his sheepshearers. Realizing that Shelah had reached maturity, and that

Judah had not fulfilled his promise, Tamar determined to take things into her own hands. By subterfuge she would force Judah, himself, to perform the levirate duty. She assumed the garb of a *qᵉdēshah*, or prostitute consecrated to the degrading worship of Astarte (cf. 38:21). Judah saw her, suggested illicit relations and promised "a kid of the goats" as her reward for the sinful act.

Tamar accepted Judah's offer on condition that he leave with her his signet, his cord, or bracelet, and the staff which he held. These objects would make the identification of their owner certain. The signet, or seal, would be positive proof that Judah was the guilty party.

When Judah sent the promised "kid of the goats," the *gᵉdēshah* was nowhere to be found. Judah did not search farther for her lest his own sin be exposed by the investigation.

e. Tamar Accused of Harlotry (38:24). As the head of the family, Judah had power of life and death (cf. 31:32). Tamar was betrothed to Shelah, and betrothal was considered to be as binding as marriage. When the report came to Judah that Tamar was with child as a result of harlotry, he self-righteously insisted that she be brought forth and burned.

f. Tamar Reveals the Truth (38:25-26). Displaying the signet, cord, and staff, Tamar declared that their owner was the father of her child. Judah acknowledged that he had been wrong in not observing the levirate marriage principle. The method she took to maintain her cause was a wrong one, but Judah recognized that he had treated her in an unjust manner in the matter of her marriage to Shelah.

g. Tamar's Children (38:27-30). Twin boys, Zerah and Perez, were born to Tamar. The scarlet thread placed on the hand of Zerah indicated that he had the rights and responsibilities of the firstborn. Perez appears in Matthew 1:2 as an ancestor of David, hence of Christ, Himself.

3. Joseph and Potiphar's Wife (39:1-23). It is characteristic of Joseph that his faithfulness to God results in his blessing and the blessing of those associated with him. The righteous, however, are frequently called on to suffer. The fact that Joseph loved God and that he was destined to accomplish God's will in Egypt did not cause him to be spared the terrors of false accusation and unjust imprisonment. Joseph was to learn that "all things work together for good to them that love God" (Romans 8:28).

a. Joseph, the Trusted Servant (39:1-6). Potiphar (cf. 37:26) was happy to find in Joseph a servant who could be entrusted with responsibility. Having proved himself as a slave, Joseph rose in influence until he was made overseer of Potiphar's household. Joseph had responsibility for all of the business of the household except for food (cf. 43:32). An Egyptian would consider himself defiled if he were to eat with a foreigner.

b. Joseph Tempted (39:7-12). The wife of Potiphar, attracted by the physical beauty of Joseph, proposed a sinful relationship. Joseph refused. From the human standpoint, Joseph could not betray the trust which Potiphar had placed in him. Yet Joseph had a higher motivation in his refusal: "How, then, can I do this great wickedness and sin against God?"

From day to day Potiphar's wife tempted Joseph. He remained steadfast in his refusal. On one occasion, finding herself alone with Joseph, she took hold of his garment in making her sinful suggestion. Joseph escaped, leaving the garment in her hand.

c. Joseph Falsely Accused (39:13-19). Angered at Joseph's refusal to accept her advances, Potiphar's wife determined to punish him. She called for the men of the house, who would be jealous of Joseph's position in any event. She spoke of Joseph as a Hebrew, making use of Egyptian racial prejudice. An alien Asiatic had no place in the home of an Egyptian! Her story was the reverse of the truth. According to her account Joseph had been the aggressor, and she had resisted his advances, calling for help, and seizing his garment when he fled. When Potiphar heard this report he was angered and caused Joseph to be imprisoned. It has been suggested that he might have had some doubt about his wife's story, otherwise Joseph would have been put to death.

The Egyptian *Tale of the Two Brothers* forms an interesting parallel to the temptation of Joseph. In that story it is the younger brother who is falsely accused by the older brother's wife. The wicked wife is slain by her husband when the truth is finally known.

d. Joseph in Prison (39:20-23). In prison, as in the household of Potiphar, Joseph proved himself trustworthy, and was assigned a position of responsibility. The keeper of the prison placed him over the other prisoners. Once more we see that the Lord was with Joseph. In the place of adversity, he enjoyed God's blessing. Joseph reminds us that the righteous may suffer but they can never escape the love of God.

4. Joseph and the Prisoners (40:1-23). The chief butler (Hebrew *mashqeh*, "one who gives drink") and the chief baker were important officials in the Egyptian court. Those responsible for the food and drink of the Pharaoh held positions of responsibility. The frequency of court intrigue made it necessary to have trusted individuals in these offices. The Egyptian titles of these offices would be "scribe of the sideboard" and "superintendent of the bakehouse." For an unspecified reason the individuals holding these offices fell out of favor with the reigning Pharaoh and were imprisoned with Joseph.

One evening the chief butler and the chief baker dreamed dreams which perplexed them. Joseph, who insisted that "interpretations belong to God" (40:8) suggested that they tell their respective dreams. In each case Joseph interpreted the dream, and the interpretation proved correct within the appointed time.

The chief butler dreamed of a vine with three branches, the clusters of which produced ripe grapes. In the dream the butler pressed the grapes into Pharaoh's cup. As "scribe of the sideboard" he had been responsible for Pharaoh's food and drink. The dream was in accord with his usual employment.

Joseph interpreted the dream as meaning that the chief butler would be restored to his office within three days. He asked the chief butler to remember him when restored to the position of trust in the court. Joseph mentions having been "stolen away" out of the land of the Hebrews (verse 15), a reminder that he was not a slave from birth. He does not mention the incident with Potiphar's wife, but does protest his innocency: "I have done nothing that they should put me in this dungeon."

Encouraged by the interpretation of the chief butler's dream, the chief baker related his experience of the preceding night. He saw, in his dream, three bread baskets on his own head. Baked food for Pharaoh was arranged on the top basket, but the birds devoured the food in the basket. Bread baskets such as those described here appear in tomb paintings from ancient Egypt.

The interpretation of the chief baker's dream was the opposite of that of the chief butler. Within three days the chief baker would be decapitated and impaled, becoming food for the birds of prey. To an Egyptian, who deemed the welfare of the soul in the next life dependent on the preservation of the body, such an idea would be particularly offensive.

91

On the third day, as Joseph had prophesied, the Pharaoh staged a great birthday celebration. The chief butler was restored to his office, and the chief baker was hanged.

The chief butler, in the enjoyment of his restored position, forgot Joseph and the prison episode. Later, in a time of crisis for Pharaoh, he remembered the one who had so accurately interpreted dreams.

5. Pharaoh's Dreams and Joseph's Promotion (41:1-57). Joseph, for all his innocence, remained in prison for two years. God frequently allows his faithful children to suffer, but they may be assured that His purposes are gracious.

a. Pharaoh's Dreams (41:1-8). The dreams of Pharaoh were used to bring Joseph to his attention and to emphasize God's care for Egypt and the surrounding nations. In the acts of divine Providence, much remains inexplicable. God's grace toward mankind, however, is a recurring theme of Scripture. The center of Biblical history is the family of Israel, yet Egypt became a means for providing sustenance for Jacob and his sons.

In his first dream, Pharaoh was standing by the Nile River, upon which the life of Egypt depends. Irrigation comes to the soil of Egypt by the annual overflow of the Nile. Apart from the Nile, Egypt would be a part of the great desert which covers northern Africa.

Pharaoh saw, coming from the Nile, seven fat "kine" or cows, which fed on the reed grass at the river bank. Following these, Pharaoh saw seven lean cows which stood on the banks of the river before devouring the fat cows.

In a second dream, Pharaoh saw seven good ears of "corn" (grain) followed by seven thin ears which swallowed up the good ones.

Troubled by his dreams, Pharaoh called for the wise men of his realm to interpret the dreams. The magicians, (hartumîm) or "sacred scribes," were unable to suggest an interpretation. The Septuagint identifies the magicians as *hierogrammateis*, "men versed in sacred writings." They doubtless used such arts as astrology in their efforts to predict the future.

b. The Butler's Confession (41:9-13). The butler recalled the prison episode in which Joseph had correctly interpreted his own dream and that of the chief baker. The Hebrew "servant to the captain of the guard" might be able to aid Pharaoh in his perplexity.

c. Joseph Summoned to Pharaoh (41:14-24). Joseph was quickly removed from the dungeon and prepared for his encounter with Pharaoh. As a Semite he wore a beard, but he was shaved in anticipation of his meeting the Egyptian king. Suitable clothing was provided, and Joseph was ushered into the royal presence.

With a minimum of ceremony, the king quickly related to Joseph the contents of his dreams.

d. Joseph Interprets the Dreams (41:25-32). Discounting any personal psychic powers ("what God is about to do he hath declared unto Pharaoh"), Joseph interpreted the dreams of the cattle and the ears as descriptive of the immediate future of Egypt. The seven good cattle and the seven good ears represented years of plenty. They were followed by the seven thin cattle and the seven bad ears, which represented years of famine. God was warning Pharaoh to prepare during the years of plenty for the famine which would inevitably follow.

e. Joseph's Recommendations (41:33-36). Joseph suggested that Pharaoh appoint an administrator who would be responsible for securing sufficient food during the years of plenty to provide for the needs which would arise during the famine years. One fifth of the produce of the good years was to be placed in the royal granaries for distribution during the lean years.

f. Joseph's Promotion (41:37-46). The pharaoh recognized in Joseph the kind of administrator who was needed to serve Egypt in the impending time of crisis. Joseph was appointed Grand Vizier, or Prime Minister ("over my house" 41:40). The official signet ring was given to Joseph so that he could issue edicts in the name and with the seal of the pharaoh. Egyptian fine linen was used in the clothing of Joseph. It is the material used by the royal family and the highest officials of the realm. The "gold chain" was given by the Egyptian Pharaoh when someone was to be particularly honored. It served as a kind of "distinguished service" metal.

Joseph rode in the second chariot, next to that of the pharaoh. A herald went before Joseph, crying out *Abrech*. The word is Egyptian, and has been translated in many ways. The Brown, Driver and Briggs edition of Gesenius' *Lexicon* offers seven suggested explanations. It probably is derived from Egyptian words which might be freely translated "Pay attention!"

The command of Pharaoh, "Without thee shall no man lift up his hand or his foot," is a universalism. It is tantamount to saying, "Without thee shall no man do anything."

Joseph was given an Egyptian name, Zaphenath-paneah. Its derivation is uncertain. Egyptologists suggest a meaning of "The god speaks and he (i.e. the newborn child) lives." The name would be meaningless in Hebrew. He took as his wife an Egyptian named Asenath ("She is of Neith" — an Egyptian goddess), the daughter of Poti-phera ("He whom Re [the sun god] gave"), a priest at On (Heliopolis, "the city of the sun").

g. Joseph's Administration (41:47-57). Joseph served efficiently in his office as Grand Vizier. The food was stored up in the years of plenty, so that there was no real need in the years of famine. Other countries which had been affected by the famine sent emissaries to Egypt, where they were referred to Joseph for help.

During the years of plenty, Asenath gave birth to two sons. The first was named Manasseh ("Making to forget" i.e., the trials of his earlier days), the second, Ephraim ("Fruitful" because of the blessings of God upon Joseph in Egypt). These sons of Joseph were later adopted by Jacob. They became Israelite tribes.

6. The First Visit of Joseph's Brothers (42:1-38). Back in Canaan the famine reached Jacob's home. It was rumored that grain was available in Egypt. Jacob sent an expedition to bring back food for his household.

a. Jacob Sends Ten Sons to Egypt (42:1-5). In sending an expedition to Egypt in quest of grain, Jacob determined to keep Benjamin with him. Benjamin was the youngest of his sons, and (so far as Jacob knew) the only surviving son of his favorite, Rachel. Jacob was determined that Benjamin should be kept from possible harm.

b. Joseph and his Brothers (42:6-28). When the ten brothers appeared before Joseph, he recognized them at once. They, of course, had no idea that their brother occupied a position of influence in Egypt. After questioning them concerning their home, Joseph accused them of being spies. In defending themselves they told Joseph about their home, their father, and their younger brother. Benjamin was Joseph's only full brother, a fact which accounts for Joseph's special interest in him. Joseph might have suspected that, as his brothers had once plotted to get rid of him, so Benjamin might have become a second object of their hatred.

Keeping Simeon as a hostage, Joseph insisted that the brothers should bring Benjamin to him as a proof of the truthfulness of their account of themselves. In the meantime their vessels were filled with grain, and the brothers' money was returned to the sacks in which it had been carried to Egypt.

c. The Report to Jacob (42:29-38). When the sons reported their Egyptian adventure to Jacob, the old patriarch experienced the bitterest sorrow. Convinced that Joseph and Simeon were dead, he rejected the thought of allowing Benjamin to be exposed to danger. Reuben's offer: "Thou shalt slay my two sons, if I bring him not to thee," offers no solution. The offer, however, is meaningful in the context of the ancient Near East. If a man is responsible for the death of another man's daughter, his daughter is put to death, according to the Code of Hammurabi.

7. The Second Visit of Joseph's Brothers (43:1—45:24). Reluctant as Jacob was to part with Benjamin, the threat of starvation forced him to act. Judah took the leadership in arranging the details of the trip.

a. The Arrangements (43:1-14). Facing the inevitable, Jacob agreed to permit his sons to make a second trip to Egypt in quest of grain. Careful arrangements were made. Benjamin was taken along, and Judah pledged that he would be personally responsible for his safety. Certain Canaanite delicacies, including date honey and pistacio nuts, balm, laudanum, and almonds, were taken as a gift for Joseph. These small gifts are called "the best fruits in the land" (literally, "the song of the land" — the things for which the land was famous). The money which had been found in the sacks after the first journey was to be returned, and money for a second supply of grain was carried along to Egypt.

b. The Brothers before Joseph (43:15-34). When Joseph learned of the presence of his brothers he arranged to dine with them at noon. The brothers feared the invitation, remembering the money which had been restored to their sacks. They explained the matter to the steward of Joseph's house, who assured them that all was well.

Simeon was brought out to meet his returned brothers. They, meanwhile, made ready the present which they had brought for Joseph. When Joseph arrived he was particularly solicitous for Benjamin, his full brother. Honoring Egyptian attitudes toward eating with strangers, Joseph arranged the meal for his brothers, but he dined alone. The brothers were seated according to age, a fact which caused them to "marvel" at the knowledge of this Egyptian. A five-fold portion was provided for Benjamin. This may have served as a test to determine whether or not the brothers were envious of Benjamin, as they had once been of Joseph. The brothers were impressed by the table arrangement and doubtless perplexed at Joseph's behavior. Otherwise nothing unusual is noted in connection with the dinner.

c. The Brothers Sent Homeward (44:1-10). Joseph ordered his steward to fill the sacks with grain, restore the money of his brothers, and place a silver divining cup in the bag of Benjamin. The presence of the cup would give the impression that Benjamin was a thief. The older brothers would be tested to determine whether or not they were ready to abandon Benjamin to his fate. It has also been suggested that Joseph actually planned on keeping Benjamin, his full brother, with him in Egypt. The cup would provide the excuse for separating him from his half brothers.

When the caravan was overtaken in its trek toward Canaan, the brothers properly insisted on their integrity. They suggested the death penalty as the punishment to be inflicted on the one with whom the cup might be found.

d. The Divining Cup Found (44:11-13). According to plan, the Egyptians found the cup in Benjamin's sack. Dismay fell upon the brothers. Their chief concern was for their father. They knew that the loss of Benjamin would probably bring about Jacob's speedy death.

The use of the divining cup is well attested in antiquity. Water was placed in a cup, after which particles of gold, silver, precious stones, or oil would be added. The designs thus formed were used in prophesying future events. Joseph's use of a divining cup appears incongruous with his faith in the God of Israel. Before Pharaoh he disclaimed all knowledge of the future save as God had revealed it unto him (41:16). God could have used the divining cup as a means of revelation. It is more probable, however, that Joseph's use of the cup was a part of the disguise designed to remove any suspicions from his brothers concerning his identity. It is not necessary to defend Joseph for associating himself with Egyptian superstition. Scripture does not imply that Joseph was faultless. It presents him as a good but fallible man through whom the divine purposes were carried out.

e. Judah's Offer of Himself to Bear Benjamin's Punishment (44:14-34). Joseph expressed a willingness to dismiss the ten older brothers, determining to keep Benjamin as his "bondman." Judah, however, responded with a heart-rending plea. He recounted the sorrows of Jacob. The life of Jacob was bound to that of Benjamin, and failure to bring Benjamin back would surely result in Jacob's death. Judah offered to personally remain as Joseph's bondman, urging that Benjamin be allowed to return home to his father.

f. Joseph Reveals Himself to his Brothers (45:1-15). In spite of the apparent hardness of Joseph, he was really a tender-hearted man. His earlier concern for his father and the then absent Benjamin was evidence of this. Now the pathetic plea of Judah proved too much for Joseph. He asked that all his attendants leave. In one of the most touching scenes of Scripture, Joseph made himself known to his brothers. He gave them no word of reproof. God had brought him to Egypt "to preserve life." Joseph had been made an *ab* unto Pharaoh. This Hebrew word, usually translated "father" is the exact transliteration of an Egyptian word meaning "vizier," or prime minister.

Joseph not only recognized the divine will in his life in Egypt, but he rejoiced in the fact that he was able to provide for his aged father and his brothers as a result of the blessings of God. The brothers were sent on their way with orders to tell Jacob of Joseph's welfare, inviting him to join Joseph in Egypt for the years of famine which remained.

g. Pharaoh and Joseph Send for Jacob (45:16-24). The pharaoh was happy to learn that the family of his honored vizier had visited Egypt. He ordered that wagons be prepared to bring Jacob and his family into Egypt. Much of their property would be left behind in Canaan, but the wealth of Egypt was put at their disposal. Clothing and money were provided for all, with special consideration for Benjamin.

8. Jacob's Journey to Egypt (45:25—46:27).

a. Jacob Receives the News (45:25-28). The news that Joseph was still alive seemed too good to be true. Jacob had come to expect the worst, but now he had but one desire — to see Joseph again. The brothers doubtless told him of their treatment of Joseph, but Jacob could readily forgive them now that he knew that Joseph was alive. Jacob's early life had been one of deceit. He had, in turn, been deceived. Now, however, he could look forward to seeing his beloved Joseph.

b. Jacob Travels to Egypt (46:1-7). At Beer-sheba, Jacob offered sacrifices and sought to learn the will of God in the

97

matter of his going down to Egypt. God assured him, in a night vision, that he should go to Egypt. God promised to protect him, and make of him a great nation in Egypt. Jacob would not personally ever leave Egypt, for Joseph would "put his hand upon" his eyes there, closing his father's eyelids at death. Nevertheless, Jacob through his seed would become a great nation, in God's time returning to the land of Canaan.

c. Jacob's Family Which Came to Egypt (46:8-27). The list of Jacob's descendants given here may be compared with those in Numbers 26 and I Chronicles 2-8. Some of the names assume variant forms in the different lists.

9. Joseph's Settlement of his Family in Goshen (46:28—47:12).

a. Joseph Welcomes Jacob (46:28-33). Joseph came out to meet his aged father. A joyous reunion took place. Joseph then prepared to bring the news of Jacob's arrival to Pharaoh. The civilized Egyptians looked down upon the nomadic shepherds of Palestine. Goshen, however, was a part of the land of Egypt which would be particularly suitable for the semi-nomadic patriarchal tribes. Pharaoh had expressed his willingness to settle Jacob's family in this fertile area of northeastern Egypt.

b. Joseph Introduces Jacob to Pharaoh (47:1-12). The relations between Pharaoh and Jacob were most cordial. Jacob and his sons were permitted to settle "in the best of the land, in the land of Rameses." "Rameses" was so named in the reign of Rameses II. The reference to Rameses appears to be an editorial note to identify the land in which Israel sojourned to a later generation.

10. Joseph's Administration of Egypt (47:13-27). In contrast to the happy condition of Joseph's father and brothers in the land of Goshen, the Biblical record next depicts the conditions of privation in Egypt. In need of food, the Egyptians presented themselves to Joseph to explain their plight. On the first such occasion, Joseph purchased their cattle, granting them an allowance of food in exchange for horses, flocks, herds, and asses.

When the Egyptians presented themselves to Joseph again they had nothing to exchange for food except their lands. Thereupon Joseph secured the lands of the Egyptians for Pharaoh in exchange for a food allowance. The priests were exempted because they received an allotment of food at Pharaoh's expense

The purchase of land by Joseph introduced a feudal system of land tenure. Seed was allotted to the Egyptians, with the understanding that one-fifth of the produce of the land would revert to Pharaoh.

Although this act of Joseph involved a measure of humiliation, including the surrender of lands to the state, it made possible a strong central government which could take measures to prevent famine conditions. The life of Egypt depends upon the Nile, and all of the inhabitants of the Nile Valley must co-operate if the water is to be used efficiently. The government was in a position to regulate the use of Nile water and also to begin a system of artificial irrigation by means of canals which could carry the waters of the Nile to otherwise inaccessible areas.

Joseph's economic policy is described, with no hint as to either approval or censure. Some have thought that Joseph drove a "hard bargain" and took advantage of the conditions to enhance the power of the throne. That the emergency resulted in a centralization of authority is clear. There is no hint that Joseph, personally, profited from the situation, however. On the contrary, the people said to Joseph, "Thou hast saved our lives" (47:25). Many, doubtless, resented the necessity of being moved, but in famine conditions it was necessary to bring the population to the store cities where food was available. Convenience must be forgotten in a life-and-death situation such as Egypt faced.

The "tax" of a fifth of the produce of the fields was not excessive according to ancient standards. In the time of the Maccabees, the Jews paid the Syrian government one-third of the seed (I Maccabees 10:30).

Egyptologists tell us that large landed estates were owned by the nobility and the governors of the nomes ("states") during the Old Empire period (c. 3000-1900 B. C.). By the New Kingdom (after 1550 B. C.) power was centralized in the person of the Pharaoh. Joseph, as Prime Minister was instrumental in hastening this process.

11. The Last Days of Jacob (47:28—50:14). Although the years of Jacob's sojourn in Egypt were marked by economic disaster for the Egyptians, the Israelites enjoyed the blessing of God and the favor of the reigning Pharaoh. The last years of Jacob's life were happy ones. In earlier life he had both deceived and been deceived. Trials had come his way. His beloved Rachel was buried at Bethlehem. But his last days were days of tranquility. Joseph was alive, and the family was prospering in Egypt.

a. Jacob's Request concerning His Burial (47:27-31). At the end of a stormy life, Jacob expressed a desire for burial in

99

Canaan rather than Egypt. Jacob was the heir to the promises which had been made to Abraham and Isaac. Canaan was the land which God had promised as their inheritance. Egypt served as a refuge in a time of famine, but Jacob insisted that his bones be taken back to the land of his fathers. Joseph was asked to take a solemn oath (cf. 24:2) that his father's wishes be honored. This he willingly did.

Realizing that his last days were approaching, and thankful that Joseph had assured him of a burial in Canaan, Jacob, or Israel as he is here named, "bowed down upon the bed's head" (47:31). He apparently turned over on his bed, and bent his head toward the head of the bed, as if to prostrate himself before God in worship. The Septuagint, followed in Hebrews 11:21, suggests a different pointing of the Hebrew words, reading "bowed himself upon the top of his staff." According to this reading, which is followed by the Syriac, Jacob used his staff to raise himself in the bed and to worship, remembering God's blessings during the years of his life. The first reading, that followed by the Masoretic Text, appears to be the most natural one. Leupold suggests that the author of the Epistle to the Hebrews quoted from the Septuagint, as he usually did, without suggesting a change because no vital point was involved.

b. Jacob Blesses the Sons of Joseph (48:1-22). In the subsequent history of the nation of Israel, Joseph does not appear as one of the tribes. The historical reason for this is here indicated. Joseph became two tribes, for his sons Ephraim and Manasseh were adopted by his father Jacob, and given an inheritance among his sons.

Jacob's death did not come as quickly as was expected (47:27-31). His weak condition continued, however, and he utilized his remaining days in preparing for the end. Joseph had enjoyed a position of special favor with Jacob. For this reason, Jacob determined to adopt the two sons of Joseph. The reference to Rachel (48:7) indicates how keenly Jacob felt her loss to the day of his death. His adoption of Joseph's sons serves as a kind of tribute to her. She had but two children, Joseph and Benjamin. By adopting Joseph's sons, Rachel became the mother of three tribes: Ephraim, Manasseh, and Benjamin.

When Joseph brought his sons to his father for the blessing, Joseph brought them before Jacob in such a way that Manasseh would be at his right hand, and Ephraim at his left hand. The right hand is looked upon as the favored place, and Joseph reasoned that his elder son should be honored in this way. Jacob, however, crossed his hands so that his right hand was placed on Ephraim's head, and his left hand on the head of Manasseh. When Joseph objected, Jacob insisted that blessings would be meted out to both sons, but Ephraim would be the greater of the two.

While the blessings upon Ephraim and Manasseh are of a general nature, Jacob mentions a specific plot of ground which he allotted to Joseph. This is described as "one portion (*shekem,* shoulder) . . . which I took out of the hand of the Amorite with my sword and with my bow" (48:22). This battle is not mentioned elsewhere in Genesis. Although many commentators think that the city of Shechem is meant (in a kind of word play), the reference cannot be to the taking of Shechem in Genesis 34, an act which Jacob repudiated. Whatever the location of the plot of ground, and whatever the circumstances by which it was acquired, its identity was a matter of tradition as late as New Testament times. Sychar is described as "near to the parcel of ground that Jacob gave to his son, Joseph" (John 4:5).

The Nuzu tablets indicate that adoption was a common procedure in patriarchal times. They also show that an oral blessing, such as that pronounced by Jacob, was considered binding when contested in court. The blessing is a kind of "last will and testament." In Scriptural use, such a blessing also conveys a prophecy concerning the future. Ephraim became the strongest of the twelve tribes. In the time of the divided kingdom the name of Ephraim was frequently used as a synonym for Israel (the Northern Kingdom).

c. Jacob Blesses His Own Sons (49:1-27). In the form of poetry, a predictive blessing is pronounced by Jacob on each of his sons. Although in some cases severe censure is given, in no case is a tribe disinherited. Some of the tribes had positions of greater honor and usefulness than did others, but the Israelites remained conscious of their descent from the twelve sons of Jacob.

(1) Reuben (49:3-4). Reuben, as the first born, might be expected to fill the honored position. Reuben, however, had given evidence of instability of character. His sin with Bilhah (35:22) is mentioned as a grave offence in Jacob's eyes. Reuben forfeited his privileges as the first-born of Jacob. The tribe of Reuben is rarely mentioned in subsequent Israelite history.

101

It occupied territory to the east of the Dead Sea, north of Moab. The Moabites early encroached on its territory.

(2) Simeon and Levi (49:5-7). Simeon and Levi are the second and third sons of Jacob by Leah. They shared in the treachery against Hamor and Shechem described in Genesis 34. For this reason Jacob prophesies that they will be divided and scattered. Simeon's inheritance was taken out of the land assigned to Judah (cf. Joshua 19:1-9). Simeon was ultimately absorbed into Judah so that it lost its separate tribal existence.

The tribe of Levi was dispersed throughout the land with no distinct tribal inheritance (cf. Joshua 21:1-40). The Levites did, however, serve as ministers of the sanctuary and teachers of Israel. Aaron and the priestly line which is traceable to him come from Levi.

In the case of Levi, Jacob's prophecy was literally fulfilled, but a place of usefulness was reached in the very dispersion of the sons of Levi.

(3) Judah (49:8-12). In contrast to the words addressed to Reuben, Simeon, and Levi, Jacob uttered words of enthusiastic approval of Judah. His tribe would be that which would rule in Israel. Enemies would be subdued before him. David, the king, came from the tribe of Judah. Jesus traced his lineage through David to Abraham (Matthew 1:1).

Verse ten has been interpreted Messianically from antiquity, both in the church and in the synagogue. Its exact import, however, is most difficult to determine. The reading "Until Shiloh come" dates from the German translation of Sebastian Munster (1534). Shiloh is generally taken as a name for the Messiah, meaning "Man of Rest" or "Giver of Rest." According to this view the entire passage implies that Judah's rule will culminate in a Messianic ruler who will achieve perfect rest for His people.

Ancient versions (specifically the Septuagint and the Syriac) suggest a reading "Until he that is his shall come," or "Until he come whose (it is)." This is the basis for the rendering of the Revised Standard Version: "until he comes to whom it belongs." This understanding of the text would imply that sovereignty would not depart from Judah until it found its fulfillment in the higher sovereignty of the Messiah. The Davidic rule anticipated the rule of "the Son of David" (Matthew 1:1).

The similarity of the word Shiloh to the city of that name has caused the translators of the Jewish Publication Society

Version to read "As long as men come to Shiloh." This is grammatically possible. Shiloh served as an important sanctuary before the days of the monarchy. It was specifically after that period, however, that Judah's rule was recognized. The dynasty of Judah's kings begins with David who made Jerusalem both political and religious center of the nation. For historical reasons this viewpoint must be rejected, although it is advocated by as able and devout a scholar as Franz Delitzsch.

Although some of the details may seem obscure, the basic idea of the prophetic blessing is clear. Judah will be the royal tribe. She will wield the scepter. Although she may experience difficult times, God will so overrule the events of history that the scepter will remain in Judah until the ideal king, the Messiah comes. He will serve as the fulfillment of the rule promised to Judah and begun by David.

Verses eleven and twelve describe the prosperity of the land of Judah enjoyed in the days of Judah's faithfulness to God. Vines are so common that they are used for tethering the ass, and wine so abundant that garments are washed in it. This does not, of course, imply that this was actually done, but that there was such abundance that there was no fear of waste.

In the same context of the enjoyment of the blessing of God is the statement concerning Judah: "His eyes are dark from wine and his teeth white from milk." There is no thought here of the bloodshot eye of the drunkard. The charge that this is "a later addition, taunting the tribe with decadence" (*Interpreter's Bible*) misses the point entirely. The emphasis is on the prosperity of the land, in which an abundance of nourishing food imparts a healthy color to the inhabitants of the land. The eyes have a ruddy darkness from the wine, and the teeth are white with milk. With this may be contrasted the curse pronounced upon the transgressor in Amos 4:6: "I also have given you cleanness of teeth in all your cities, and want of bread in all your places . . ."

The Septuagint, Vulgate, and some modern scholars interpret the adjectives as comparatives: "His eyes are more sparkling than wine and his teeth are whiter than milk." Although this reading appears less natural than that given above, it is grammatically correct. In either case, the meaning is basically the same. The land shall enjoy the blessing of abundant prosperity.

(4) Zebulun (49:13). Zebulun was Jacob's sixth son by Leah. Although playing no decisive part in the later history of Israel,

Zebulun was commended for its part in the struggle against the Canaanite, Sisera (Judges 5:18).

The favorable geographical location of Zebulun is described. In Joshua 19:10-16 the boundaries of Zebulun appear to cut it off from the Mediterranean. It is bounded on the South by Issachar, on the East and North by Naphtali, and on the West by Asher. It is possible, however, that the borders fluctuated and that Zebulun did actually reach the Mediterranean at some periods of her history.

Leupold stresses the fact that the blessing does not state that Zebulun would possess the seashore. Translating, "he shall be toward the shore where the ships come," he suggests that Zebulun's prosperity would come through contact with those whose ships touched the shore, including the Phoenicians. This would account for the reference to Zidon, which was never actually possessed by any of the tribes of Israel.

(5) Issachar (49:14-15). Jacob's fifth son by Leah, Issachar is likened to a strong, bony ass which chose a life of ease instead of one of service. The territory of Issachar included Mt. Gilboa and the fertile Esdraelon Plain (cf. Joshua 19:17-23). The very excellence of its tribal inheritance proved a snare. Issachar submitted to the yoke of the foreigner rather than leave its ploughshare. In Judges 1:27-33 the Canaanites are observed as maintaining a foothold in Northern Israel. In Issachar it appears that they actually retained the supremacy.

(6) Dan (49:16-18). Dan, the first son of Bilhah, Rachel's handmaid, occupied territory northwest of Jerusalem, including the sea-port of Joppa. The inhabitants of the land, including the Amorites (Judges 1:34) contested the claim of the Danites to their inheritance, with the result that a portion of the tribe migrated to the territory around Leshem, or Laish (Judges 18:7, 27ff.). This became the northern Dan, frequently mentioned as the northern limit of the land of Israel ("from Dan to Beer-sheba").

Jacob's blessing implies that Dan, although small, "will judge his people," i.e., maintain its independence and defend the members of the tribe from the pressure of its foes.

Dan is likened to a "horned snake," a small but highly venomous serpent. When disturbed, the "horned snake" darts out upon any passing animal. Similarly Dan was to wage guerilla warfare with its foes, bringing about their destruction.

(7) Gad (49:19). Gad was the first son of Leah's handmaid,

104

Zilpah. His territory was east of the Jordan, north of Reuben. Ammonites, Moabites, and other desert tribes were a constant danger to Gad (cf. Judges 11).

Jacob prophesied that marauding bands would press upon the tribe of Gad. Gad, however, is seen dispersing them and pressing hard upon their heels as they retreat.

(8) Asher (49:20). Asher, Zilpah's second son, inhabited a strip of land along the Mediterranean from Mt. Carmel to the borders of Phoenicia. This was a fertile district, rich in wheat, olives, and grapes. The name Asher means "happy," and the tribe of Asher is described as prosperous and capable of producing delicacies fit for a king.

(9) Naphtali (49:21). Bilhah's second son, Naphtali, occupied the territory north of the Sea of Galilee, as far as the Lebanon Mountains. It included the fertile Plain of Gennesareth.

Jacob termed Naphtali, "a hind let loose" or "a liberated deer." The picture is that of a deer from which all restraint has been removed. Naphtali is praised for its heroism in Judges 5:18. The song of Deborah and Barak (Judges 5) is thought to exemplify the "words of beauty" or "goodly words" which Naphtali is said to speak.

Because of the difficulty of relating the two parts of the description of Naphtali, Genesis 49:21 has been emended in various ways. The Septuagint and many modern scholars suggest: "Naphtali is a slender terebinth which putteth forth goodly branches." The Revised Standard Version suggests: "Naphtali is a hind let loose, that bears comely fawns." The reading of the Masoretic Text, however, agrees with the Targums and the Samaritan Pentateuch. The suggested emendations are not convincing.

(10) Joseph (49:22-26). Rachel's firstborn, and Jacob's favorite son, the blessing on Joseph has a special significance. Its fulfillment must be sought in the "house of Joseph," or the tribes of Ephraim and Manasseh (cf. 48:8-22).

Joseph is described as "a fruitful bough" or, literally, "son of a fruitful (tree)." The word, "fruitful," *parah,* appears in the name Ephraim. It is likely that Jacob used this word play because Ephraim was to become the principal branch of the Joseph tribe.

The enmity of "the archers" appears to be a reference to the treatment which Joseph received at the hand of his brothers.

Strengthened by God, however, Joseph was able to stand firm and, ultimately, become a means of blessing to his persecutors.

The fruitfulness of Joseph, however, carries the point of reference into the future. The Joseph tribes — Ephraim and Manasseh — will be multiplied and blessed. Three blessings are specified. The "blessing of heaven above" speaks of the dew, rain, and sunshine (cf. Genesis 27:39; Deuteronomy 33:13), "blessings of the deep" or springs and fountains which bring fertility to the soil from beneath the earth, and "blessings of the breasts and of the womb," or fertility among men and animals. Hosea 9:14, in a context of impending judgment, speaks of "a miscarrying womb and dry breasts," the opposite of the blessing here described.

Although there are some textual problems in the interpretation of 49:26, its import is clear. The blessings of Joseph are greater than those received by his progenitors. Joseph will be "a prince among his brethren" (literally, "separated" from his brethren, given a position of special prestige and honor).

(11) Benjamin (49:27). Benjamin was Jacob's second son by Rachel, who died at the time of his birth. It was a small tribe, with territory north of Judah and Jerusalem. Saul, Israel's first king was a Benjamite, as was Saul of Tarsus.

The metaphor whereby Benjamin is called "a ravenous wolf" describes the warlike character of the tribe. Benjamite bowmen and slingers were famous (Judges 20:16; I Chronicles 8:40, 12:2). The description is complimentary, but it may contain a veiled warning.

d. The Death and Burial of Jacob (49:28—50:14). After blessing his sons, Jacob gave them instructions concerning his burial. He wished to be buried in the burial plot which Abraham had purchased from Ephron the Hittite, which had become the family burial place. Here we learn for the first time that Rebekah and Leah had been buried there, along with Sarah, Abraham, and Isaac.

Although much space is given to a description of the last hours of Jacob, the account of his death is brief. Jacob had evidently been sitting while giving his blessing and instructions to his sons. Now "he gathered up his feet into his bed, and expired, and was gathered unto his people." That the "gathering to his people" must not be thought of as equivalent to burial is evident from the fact that burial took place in Canaan some days after Jacob's death. Jacob died in faith, and his soul is thought of as joining his ancestors in another world. Subsequent revelation clarifies the condition of the soul of the believer after death. In Christ, life and immortality are brought to light. Even in Genesis, however, at the dawn of Israel's history, the consciousness of a continuing joyful existence is clearly indicated.

Joseph took personal charge of the arrangements for his father's funeral. His request for permission to bury his father in Canaan may have been designed to allay any suspicions as to his motive in leaving Egypt. He made it clear that the death of his father was not an excuse to leave Egypt permanently. Joseph recognized his filial responsibilities, and requested permission to perform them.

His official position in Pharaoh's court enabled Joseph to secure needed aid. Jacob's body was mummified in accord with current Egyptian methods of embalming. A period of forty days was necessary to complete the embalming procedure. A total of seventy days subsequent to Jacob's death were spent in mourning, after which Joseph, having received permission from the Pharaoh, took Jacob's body to Canaan for burial.

A large procession, including all of Jacob's sons, servants of Pharaoh, and "elders" of the land of Egypt, with chariots and horsemen, set out for Canaan with Jacob's mummified body. They paused at a place, not identified, known as the threshing-floor of Atad, where a week was spent in mourning (cf. I Samuel 31:13). The Hebrew word for mourning is *'ēbel*. The word for meadow is *'abel*. The name given to the field by the Semitic-speaking Canaanites seems to involve a word play. Abel-mizraim would normally be interpreted as "Field of Egypt." Because of the mourning of the Egyptians (and the Israelites who were with them) the Canaanites used the name Abel-mizraim in the sense of "Mourning of the Egyptians," or "the place where the Egyptians mourned." While such funeral processions would have been relatively common in Egypt, it was an unheard-of thing for Egyptians to come to Canaan to bury a dignitary.

12. The Last Years of Joseph (50:15-26). The history contained in Genesis is brought to a quick conclusion after the death of Jacob.

a. Joseph and His Brothers (50:15-21). Joseph's brothers feared that, after Jacob's death, Joseph might seek revenge for their sin against him. They stated that Jacob expressed a dying wish that Joseph forgive his brothers. Since Joseph was present at his father's death, it seems strange that he would not have

107

heard such a request. It is possible that the brothers were lying in order to make sure that Joseph would treat them kindly after Jacob's death.

Joseph insisted that judgment was in the hand of God. God had brought good out of their intended evil. Joseph stated that he would provide for his brothers and their children.

b. The Death of Joseph (50:22-26). In Egyptian writings an ideal lifetime is 110 years. Joseph lived this ideal life. He lived long enough to see Ephraim's great grandchildren. Machir was the most warlike of the clans of Manasseh (cf. Joshua 17:1; Judges 5:14; Numbers 32:39). His descendants settled in Gilead (Numbers 32:40; Deuteronomy 3:15).

Although Joseph died in Egypt, he was conscious of the fact that Canaan had been given as the inheritance of Abraham's seed. Unlike that of Jacob, Joseph's mummified body was not immediately taken to Canaan. Joseph made his kinsmen solemnly promise that, when they left Egypt for Canaan, they would bring his bones with them.

Genesis closes with the note that, after a life of one hundred and ten years, Joseph died, was embalmed, and placed in a "coffin" in Egypt. The coffin (Hebrew 'arôn, used of the "ark" of the covenant) was a mummy-case. This mummy-case remained with the Israelites through the years of bondage, exodus, and wilderness wandering. It remained a silent prophecy that God would one day bring the Israelites back to the land of their fathers. Joseph's body was taken from Egypt at the time of the exodus (Exodus 13:19), and buried in Shechem (Joshua 24:32).